THE GIFTS OF GOD

Discovering the

Heart of the Giver

MATTHEW J DUNN

To my wife and sons, who spurred me on to turn good intentions into something real.

I love you more than you know.

Contents

Acknowledgements

I joke that this book is the product of five years of hard work and procrastination in equal measure! In reality, I've spent five years discovering how and what to write through trial and error and by the encouragement, insights and support of many friends and acquaintances. I take full responsibility for any errors in this book, but must acknowledge the many people who have in various ways made positive and constructive contributions to it.

Thank you to Pastors Che & Sue Ahn for consistently encouraging me in my call to teach and for revealing the generosity of God so beautifully.

Thank you to David Bedell at Destiny Writers for kickstarting this whole journey with your writing class.

Thank you to Mark Miller for our lunchtime conversations, humor and insights on life and writing.

Thank you to all my encouragers who routinely demonstrated more confidence in me than I do in myself; chief among them are Gwen Gibson, Bill Tilney, Andy & Karen Geerken, Faith & York Liu, Charlie Huff, Liz Voll & Kuoching Ngu.

Thank you to a great many colleagues and friends at Harvest Rock church in Pasadena over the past decade, who have helped me sharpen my thinking on fivefold ministry, spiritual gifts and on the nature and generosity of God.

Thank you to Michael Brodeur (Pastors Coach) & Alex Absalom (Dandelion Resourcing) for our insightful conversations that helped opened up the vista of the Ephesians Ascension gifts. Thank you also to Andrew Dowsett - discovering your blogs on 'people-as-gifts' was like finding a treasure trove.

Thank you to Dr Mark Stibbe at The BookLab for lighting the spark to 'Write On' and for the honest and constructive review of my first draft, which has taught me that the true work of writing is re-rewriting.

Thank you to Isobel Allum for calling out the writer in me in Troon, Scotland.

Finally, thank you to everyone who told me that they would read my book, long before I'd written it. I really hope it was worth the wait.

PREFACE

I did not grow up in church.

I put my faith in Christ as a sixteen year old after spending a year desperately seeking out meaning and purpose for my life. I began attending my local Church of England congregation at the invitation of my best friend at the time. I discovered a loving community of all ages who were also seeking to live out their faith in Christ.

I played sports all through High School so my weekends generally revolved around sporting fixtures, training or resting. I rarely went to church on a Sunday morning, instead attending the Sunday evening service then staying on for youth group straight afterwards. This evening service usually followed a shortened form of the Anglican liturgy. The services were structured yet relaxed; traditional yet contemporary; intimate yet full of awe; energetic yet contemplative. This was my introduction to Church and I am forever grateful for it.

I recall numerous communion services in which we followed the liturgy, sang a traditional hymn alongside contemporary heartfelt songs of adoration while some of the ladies would dance barefoot and wave a flag, someone else might speak out in tongues and the leader would offer prayers for healing (the kind where they actually pray for healing like it could really happen) and then we shared the sign of peace with one another before reciting the communion liturgy and taking the bread and wine (real wine... that tasted like port).

These various expressions of prayer and worship were sometimes described to me as being *charismatic*. Whatever they were, it was all new to me and I loved it.

Over time, I moved away to college and continued to grow in my faith. I briefly attended a more reformed Anglican church which had great bible preaching but nobody danced or prayed for healing or prophesied. I eventually settled in a local charismatic-Baptist[1] church that became my spiritual home for twenty years. The Scriptures were preached, the worship was a heartfelt blend of traditional and contemporary, prayers for healing were common, some people prophesied and others sometimes prayed in tongues. A decade ago I moved continents to the United States and found myself in Southern California at a non-denominational pentecostal-charismatic church that was birthed in a major renewal and move of the Spirit, and have served there as a Pastor on staff for the last 8 years. The worship music style was a rock/pop blend and usually went on for an extended period of time, people would prophesy over each other routinely, healing was common, many people sang or spoke in tongues during worship and people regularly prayed for miracles. It was common to describe all these things as part of our 'charismatic' expression.

My working definition of the term 'charismatic' was that it described a church that believed in these kinds of empowered spiritual practices and whose worship seemed 'energized' by the presence of Holy Spirit. It seemed that in 'charismatic' churches there were gifts and expressions that were rarely found in more traditional churches (whatever 'traditional' means) i.e. praying for healing, prophesying, speaking in tongues, words of knowledge etc.

I was interested in these gifts and most of what I read about them or heard taught about them tended to be based on a list of about twenty five 'spiritual gifts' that could be found in the New Testament (actual numbers of gifts may go up or down depending on your denomination… terms and conditions may apply!).

For years this was my grid for understanding spiritual gifts: there's a list; they come from the Holy Spirit; anyone can have them; it's okay to ask God for various gifts; they are all important (although the Apostle Paul seemed especially enthusiastic about prophecy); they should be normal (except the weird ones). That was my theology of spiritual gifts sorted!

But there was a problem.

All these gifts were attributed to the Holy Spirit and when people claimed to be exercising one of these gifts in a particularly weird (or even harmful) way, the end result was that the Holy Spirit got the blame and people seemed to not want to talk about Holy Spirit for a while. It seemed Holy Spirit was like the awkward relative at family gatherings; they can be exciting to be around now and again but they might just buy your five year old kids fireworks when you aren't looking!

I occasionally visited churches where they would mention they believed in spiritual gifts but no-one seemed to actually use them; I visited some churches where anyone might exercise one of these gifts and leaders would offer a commentary on what was happening for people who might not be familiar to them. I visited other churches where the leaders were the ones exercising spiritual gifts in very powerful (and sometimes flamboyant) ways, often conveying a sense of their advanced spiritual zeal. I even visited a couple places where... well, it was all just a bit weird to be truthful!

And what about all the other spiritual gifts that the Bible talks about that don't seem to be valued as highly as these more 'impressive' ones? Why didn't they get talked about more? Why did nobody get excited about gifts like teaching, giving and serving?

That is why I wanted to write this book. I want to offer a fresh perspective on understanding these gifts. As we explore what the New

Testament really says about all these spiritual gifts it is also vital that we understand the character and nature of our trinitarian God who gives them. One of the myths I want to bust is that all these 'charismatic' gifts are from the Holy Spirit. Actually I believe the New Testament teaches that God, Jesus and Holy Spirit each give gifts and it's important to know where they come from. This is because the gifts reveal the heart of their Giver. We worship a trinitarian God. Gifts are not just the remit of Holy Spirit. We dishonor the unity of God when we dishonor one member of the Trinity in relation to the others; we are not faithfully worshipping God.

There are three significant passages in Paul's letters that refer to gifts of some kinds and then four other short verses that also refer to gifts. The main passages are found in Romans 12, 1 Corinthians 12-14 and Ephesians 4 with the additional material found in 1 Corinthians 7, Ephesians 3, 1 Peter 4 and Hebrews 2. In the book I will visit all these passages to see what they have to say to us.

My hope is that as you read this book you will be captivated by the generosity of our Giving God and encouraged by the ways that God is already gifting you to reflect the image and goodness of your Creator.

INTRODUCTION

The idea for this book initially came from a desire to offer an introductory class of the spiritual gifts that are listed in the New Testament. As I researched and studied familiar passages I began to uncover fresh understanding that challenged some of my existing paradigms around these so-called 'charismatic gifts'.

In my conversations with fellow believers across different church streams and traditions I began to realize that perhaps there are better ways to understand the nature of these gifts than our well worn charismatic dogma has offered.

I discovered that even using the word 'charismatic' can trigger a whole barrage of associated thoughts and beliefs, some of which are helpful and some of which can be profoundly unhelpful. Just as the word 'evangelical' now has different connotations to different groups of people (both esteemed and pejorative), so calling the gifts of God in the New Testament 'charismatic' or 'spiritual' gifts can have the same effect.

Cultures change, both inside and outside the church and this requires us to constantly refresh our ways of expressing biblical truth in order to communicate effectively with the changing culture and to allow the leaven of God's Kingdom to go to work. Vocabulary shapes culture, and periodically moments come when the shift in perspective that we are seeking requires us to change our ways of speaking about something. Words matter because *words create worlds*.

My hope therefore in this book is to go back to Scripture with fresh eyes, to see how we can better understand these gifts, their origin and purpose in a way that will encourage Christians from many different cultures and church traditions to engage with them in a fresh way that remains faithful to Scripture, accessible to all believers and above all, honoring to our Three-in-One God, who is Father, Son and Holy Spirit. It is unfortunate that whenever these gifts are abused or mis-represented it usually happens in such a way that brings disrepute to Holy Spirit who is God's divine Gift to believers (Acts 2.38).

In Part One of the book, I will take the time and space to root our paradigm for the New Testament gifts in the nature and character of God as both the ultimate Giver and the supreme Gift. If we lose sight of the generous nature of God in any discussion of spiritual gifts, then we have disconnected the gifts from the heart of the Giver. This will also keep our perspective on where the greater Gift lies, something which I fear is in danger of being lost in some charismatic church circles. It also requires us to embrace the often overlooked doctrine of 'God as Trinity' lest we accidentally separate Father, Son and Spirit from their divine unity. The gifts are meant to be a testimony to our unity with and in God. The self-giving Trinity is the Gift of God to us.

In Part Two, I will then take a fresh look at the gifts of God that are mentioned in three main passages in the New Testament. These passages are found in Paul's letters to the Roman, Corinthian and Ephesian churches, and I will consider how the context of these letters provide valuable insights into a proper understanding of what Paul is writing about. I will show how the Father, Son and Holy Spirit are *all* involved and revealed in the variety of gifts we read about, and propose the purposes for which the gifts have been given. I will also identify several other New Testament references to various gifts which are mentioned before finally offering a framework for how we can keep '*the main thing the main thing*'.

I am aware that Part One of this book might feel a bit more theological to some readers that Part Two. That will excite some readers and perhaps deter others. If this makes Part One feel a bit dry or heavy in places to you, I can only apologize for my writing style and I suggest that you jump ahead to Part Two and then come back to Part One later. I promise you there are treasures to be mined throughout the book.

PART ONE: *THE GIFT OF THE GIVER*

"Once it was the blessing, Now it is the Lord;
Once it was the feeling, Now it is His Word.
Once His gifts I wanted, Now the Giver own;
Once I sought for healing, Now Himself alone"

From a hymn by A.B. Simpson (1843-1919)

Chapter 1: GOD IS THE GIVER

*And I believe in the Holy Ghost, The Lord and giver of life, Who
proceedeth from the Father and Son, Who with the Father and the
Son together is worshiped and glorified, Who spake by the
Prophets.* (Book of Common Prayer[2])

*"Every generous act of giving, with every perfect gift, is from
above, coming down from the Father of lights, with whom there is
no variation or shadow due to change." (James 1:17 NRSV)*

'Gift': *noun.* a thing given willingly to someone without
payment; a present.

I t is in the very nature of God to be a generous giver.
This book is an exploration of God's generosity, what it looks like,
how we experience it and where it comes from.

From the first pages of the Bible at the beginning of the creation story, we read that God is the source of Creation; the one from whom
everything that was made came forth. God gave light to illuminate
the darkness and then gave life through the gift of breathing into the
first human that was made from the dusty soil of the earth. He gave
authority to humans for them to exercise dominion in his creation,
carrying his likeness.

God's humanity project in creation reveals that he gave breath (life), gave names, gave food, gave purpose and gave choice to humans. Even in the face of their subsequent rebellion against their Creator, God gave the humans clothing to cover up their nakedness.

All these things instinctively flowed out of God the Creator, because God's abundance is at the very center of the Creation project, revealing himself through his creation, putting his glory and power and wisdom and strength on display. When you consider that 'through him all things were made' and 'in him was life' (Jn 1.3-4), then it's not really surprising that every need the created order has will be met through the outflow of God's abundance.

If God exists in reality then he is not defined merely by what we think about him. God cannot be constrained by our limited thinking about the divine source of all things. Our thinking simply falls short of the reality of God. It is we who are constrained by our limited thinking, not God. I hope that this book will engage us to think about God in less limiting ways that are faithful to the reality of who he is, especially as he is revealed to us by the Scriptures.

Blessed

What is your perception of God? Do you perceive God as distant? Ethereal? Mean spirited? Perhaps you think of God as angry or vindictive. How did you form these views of God?

The mysterious Old Testament character of Job, about whom we know so little, was a prosperous man who experienced great loss (and eventually even greater prosperity). The Scripture introduces him as a man having seven sons and three daughters. He possessed 7,000 sheep, 3,000 camels, 500 yoke of oxen, 500 female donkeys and very many servants and was described as the greatest of all the people of the east (Job 1:1–3). By the measure of his day, he was a very wealthy person who would have commanded great respect, and the story teller makes sure to tell us the measure of Job's wealth.

In the very first chapter of the book of Job, we discover that his oxen and donkeys get struck down by Arabian marauders, his sheep and servants get burned up by fire that falls from heaven, his camels get slaughtered by Babylonian invaders and finally he loses all his children to a freak windstorm which demolishes the property they were staying in and kills them. In the face of this tragedy and loss, Job exclaimed 'Yahweh has given and Yahweh has taken away'.

Job recognizes that his children and his material prosperity are given to him by Yahweh, even though Job plays a participatory part in acquiring them (not to mention Mrs Job's contribution). There is no disconnection in Job's mind between being a hard-working, successful shepherd and seeing that all he has is given to him by God. He has been (and would be again) a recipient of the generosity of God even though his life carried the scars of loss and tragedy.

At the end of the book of Job, after much hand wringing and questioning from his friends as to the cause of the tragedies and loss he had experienced, Job remains submitted to Yahweh the Creator, acknowledging God's sovereignty in all things: "And the LORD gave Job twice as much as he had before… And the LORD blessed the latter days of Job more than his beginning. And he had 14,000 sheep, 6,000 camels, 1,000 yoke of oxen, and 1,000 female donkeys. He had also seven sons and three daughters." (Job 42:10, 12–13).

Job's wealth is doubled and he has more children to replace those who had tragically died. I offer this reminder of Job's story to show

how Job's view of God as a Giver remained solely dependent on his understanding of the character of God and not on his perspective of his own circumstances of abundance or lack or his experiences of loss. We may each experience loss and lack at various times in our life, but they do not define the character of God. We must be careful not to limit our view of God because of experiences like that.

Recently there has been an increasing trend on social media to use the hashtag #*blessed* to label posts. Typically these posts put on display material abundance or extravagance and use the hashtag to imply that what they have is a blessing. As with so many popular cultural trends, they may start with a good intention or kernel of truth, but they can quickly become hideous caricatures.

The kernel of truth in #*blessed* is that it is in fact biblical to acknowledge that God is an abundant giver and that it is entirely appropriate to give thanks to God for all the material wealth that has come to us. But wealth is not always created through righteous means, and wealth in itself is not always a sign of God's blessing. The bible also speaks about unjust wealth and the wealth of the wicked(e.g. Ps 73.12; Ezekiel 7.21).

Like most kingdom truths we must hold in tension that material wealth can be a sign of God's blessing, but not always. If we fail to hold the tension of this then we will either make the error of believing that all wealth is evil (this is sometimes connected to the idea that poverty is more 'spiritual', which is unbiblical), or alternatively we make the error of believing that all wealth is the measure of our favor with God (which is the worst form of the 'prosperity' gospel, which is also unbiblical).

In this regard perhaps Job was an inspiration to the apostle Paul who expresses an important lesson in Philippians 4.11-12, "for I have learned to be content whatever the circumstances". Paul is a man who has lived through more than a few challenging circumstances… stoning, beatings, imprisonment, shipwreck to name but a few. Paul goes on, "I know what it is to be in need, and I know what it is to have plenty. I have learned the secret of being content in any and every situation, whether well fed or hungry, whether living in plenty or in want. *I can do all this through him who gives me strength*" (Phil. 4:11–13 NIV). Paul knew he could trust God to give him what he needed at just the right time, because Paul was confident in God's nature as a giver.

I can do all this through him who gives me strength!

I have heard this verse misused by Christians so many times. Usually it gets used as some kind of Christian good luck mantra to justify our own endeavors… as if muttering this verse will imbue me with the power to succeed at my latest project.

But Paul is writing in the context of his radical obedience to the mission that God had given him to take the Gospel to the Gentiles and to stand before Kings and rulers. Paul gave his life to this mission after his dramatic encounter with the risen Lord Jesus, and he can persevere in it through every challenge and setback because he has confidence that God will give him the strength to continue, whether he has plenty or is experiencing lack. Paul has discovered the secret of being #*blessed*.

Just in time delivery

I spent the first fifteen years of my working life in the construction industry. In my work as a structural engineer both the design team and the constructors have to work together to consider how something will actually be constructed. It's great having a beautifully aesthetic building on paper or a super efficient structural frame design but they are useless if they cannot be built safely and efficiently.

One of the construction logistics techniques that enabled constructors to build projects on especially constrained city center sites that had virtually no space to store materials was called 'just-in-time' delivery. In other words, construction materials and components were delivered to site when they were needed and not before... 'just-in time'! This ensured that the materials didn't take up valuable space on the constrained site, rather they could be lifted straight into place in the construction. It requires careful planning and logistics.

In the Old Testament we read about a father of our faith who experienced the gift of God's provision 'just in time'. I am referring to Abraham. God made a covenant with Abraham beginning in Genesis 12. God promised Abraham numerous offspring. After a very long wait to have children, including a foolish attempt to force the issue with Abraham's wife's female servant, God indeed gives Abraham a son called Isaac. When Isaac is a young man, God speaks to Abraham in Genesis 22 and instructs him to take Isaac, his only son, and to offer him as a sacrifice at Mt Moriah. The story is thick with mystery and imagery for us today, but it is also shocking, quite apart from the idea of child sacrifice, because Isaac is the promised son of Abraham given by God in fulfillment of his covenant promise, so to ask for him to be sacrificed seems contrary to everything that God has been promising to Abraham in terms of having numerous offspring. Isaac is the sum total of Abraham's promised offspring.

In the astonishing climax to the narrative in Genesis 22, Abraham prepares a wood pile for an altar and with Isaac bound to it, Abraham raises his knife ready to kill Isaac, his son of promise, when God dramatically intervenes... just in time!

> *[The angel of the Lord] said, "Do not lay your hand on the boy or do anything to him, for now I know that you fear God, seeing you have not withheld your son, your only son, from me." And Abraham lifted up his eyes and looked, and behold, behind him was a ram, caught in a thicket by his horns. And Abraham went and took the ram and offered it up as a burnt offering instead of his son. So Abraham called the name of that place, "The LORD will provide"; as it is said to this day, "On the mount of the LORD it shall be provided.""* (Gen 22.12–14 ESV)

God gave an alternative offering for Abraham... just in time. As a result Abraham names the place of that sacrifice, 'God will provide'. In a couple of English translations, they translate the place name as 'the Lord sees' meaning that the Lord *sees the need* and *sees to it* that the need was met (see the Message, the Schocken Bible and New English Translation of the Septuagint). God is seen in that place through his gift, his provision.

God gives Abraham exactly what he needs... just in time... at just the right time. We worship a God who is both generous and timely.

(By the way, we are not told about Isaac's reaction to all this, but we should note that God is rather unsurprisingly referred to as the Fear of Isaac on two occasions in Genesis 31. I don't pretend to try and understand the nature of Isaac's relationship with God after this!)

God gives good things

One day, while teaching the Sermon on the Mount, Jesus said to the gathered crowd of listeners: "If you then, who are evil, know how to give good gifts to your children, how much more will your Father who is in heaven give good things to those who ask him!" (Matt. 7:11).

Jesus uses a tool common among ancient teachers. He sets up a concept that his listeners can easily relate to (in this case, a father providing good things for his children), and then contrasts God to that idea. It helps the listeners anchor themselves to a reference point as Jesus reveals things that they have not understood before. Jesus contrasts the listeners to God. The listeners are limited by their humanity and sinfulness, yet are still capable of being good and generous fathers. By comparison God is infinitely good and therefore both capable and willing to extend far greater generosity in providing good things when asked. Why then would we doubt it?

This confidence in the character of God and his generous nature should underpin our study of God's gifts. We are not 'entitled' to God's goodness, as if it his dutiful response to something within us, but rather we should have confidence in his goodness and generosity because it is an overflow of something within God: it flows from his own abundance and his love for the work of his own creation.

In her book *Walking in the Dust of Rabbi Jesus,* author Lois Tverberg proposes that we should maybe even have something like 'chutzpah' when we come to God… a somewhat brazen, ballsy attitude, based on our conviction of the goodness and generosity of God.

When Jesus encounters people who demonstrate this brazen confidence (*chutzpah*) in the generous nature of God he seems to celebrate them, whether it is Martha expressing faith after her brothers death, or a centurion expressing faith over his paralyzed servant (read John 11 & Matthew 8). We can have faith in the unchanging nature of God, indeed we are expected to.

God exists in a realm of abundance where there is no lack (we often refer to this divine realm as *heaven*). God is the supreme Giver, who cannot help but be generous. It is who he is. It is how he is.

In his book, *The Return of the Prodigal Son*, Henri Nouwen writes,

> *In order to become like the Father, I must be as generous as the Father is generous. Just as the Father gives his very self to his children, so must I give my very self to my brothers and sisters. Jesus makes it very clear that it is precisely this giving of self that is the mark of the true disciple[3].*

May our minds be renewed to see God more fully as he truly is. Amen.

Chapter 2: GOD IS THE GIFT

It is easy to want things from the Lord and yet not want the Lord Himself; as though the gift could ever be preferable to the Giver. (St Augustine of Hippo[4])

"I will dwell among the people of Israel and will be their God. And they shall know that I am the LORD their God, who brought them out of the land of Egypt that I might dwell among them. I am the LORD their God." (Exod 29.45–46 ESV)

"And I heard a loud voice from the throne saying, "Behold, the dwelling place of God is with man. He will dwell with them, and they will be his people, and God himself will be with them as their God" (Rev 21.3 ESV)

When I first started writing this book, I confess I was very focused on examining the traditional list of 'spiritual' gifts that are listed in the New Testament. In fact, that was where most of my attention and study was directed. However, the more I studied and reflected on these gifts and their purpose the more I began to reflect on the way that the triune God (Father, Son and Holy Spirit) give *themselves* unreservedly as a gift to us.

The gospel of John famously announces to us, *'God so loved the world that he gave his only Son'*. This self-less giving of God's self, in the person of Jesus Christ, is the ultimate expression of God's love for the world and that is what I find so amazing about the way God gives. God gives Gods-self as a gift. Granted, there are many things he gives as gifts that are not directly himself, but God primarily gives himself as the greatest expression of his love and generosity.

This thought forced me to return to the often overlooked truth of God being trinitarian in nature, or three-persons-in-one. As the early church developed their theology (often by realizing that something was wrong with the way they were talking about God), they developed Creeds which are statements of orthodoxy (right thinking) about God. Several early church creeds were written in response to heretical ideas that were being taught at the time. For example, one heretical idea was that Jesus is not divine; another was that Jesus is just God in disguise as a human, rather than being co-existent with God as a separate person. One of the first things that was solidified in these early Creeds was the idea that Christians worship only one God, but that God is three persons; Father, Son and Holy Ghost.

While most Christians would nod their head to these historic orthodox three-in-one creeds, my sense is that many Christians today are either functional polytheists worshipping three separate Gods (called Father, Jesus and Holy Spirit) or practical unitarians, choosing only to relate to one of the Father, Son or Holy Spirit depending on their own preferences about which one is 'nicest'.

Jesus the Son, is no more or less God than Father and Holy Spirit and is also one with the Father. Jesus is eternally begotten of the Father. The Holy Spirit proceeds from the Father and the Son.

This is indeed a mystery that the church has wrestled with since it's inception. In the following chapters, I simply want to point to how each *person* of the tri-une God-head is themselves given as a gift.

The gift of 'God as Creator'

The Old Testament reveals Israel's God as the Creator. The Scriptures reveal that God is the source behind the created cosmos that gives it both purpose and order. God gives form and function to the Created universe. By establishing order in Creation, the biblical account found in Genesis 1 describes how Israel's God is different from the gods worshipped by other ancient peoples who had their own chaotic creation stories.

Other ancient cultures portrayed the creation of the world as being the result of divine violence, or cosmic refuse without purpose or meaning. Israel's God, however, is shown to create with artistry and skill, embedding purpose into all that is created. The climax of the Creation story is God resting on the Sabbath to delight in all that has been created.

Trusting God as Creator means that there is predictability in the sun coming up each day, for the seasons to cycle through the year, for the rain to fall and for the sun to shine and for the harvest to come. Much of Israel's story is connected to the cycle of the seasons and the provision for the people through the land bearing its fruit and harvest. God is over his creation, intimately involved in it, but not in a way that prevents people from screwing it up! He is not distant like the god of the deists, a clockmaker who winds up the universe like a machine and then steps back to watch it unfold with no further involvement. And yet God's generosity (his blessing) can be opposed when his people act contrary to the order that has been set up in his creation.

We can read the creation account of Genesis 1 in many different ways. One straightforward reading is to note how life on earth is designed for fruitfulness and reproduction, whether it is the seeds of the plant world or the multiplication of fish in the sea of animals on the land and air. The Creation that God fashions has the expectation of multiplication built into it, because it reflects the nature of it's maker.

It is these characteristics of God's nature, his abundance and generosity, that are present in the biblical idea of 'blessing'. To bless in the OT means "to endue with power for success, prosperity, fecundity, longevity, etc." (Source: *Theological Wordbook of the Old Testament*) and throughout the book of Genesis the idea of blessing seems to be equated with increase, fruitfulness and abundance.

In the Genesis Creation project, God's first blessing is recorded on the fifth day. It is pronounced over the animals that had been created to occupy the seas and the sky: 'God blessed them saying, "be fruitful and increase in number and fill the water in the seas and let the birds increase on the earth"' (Gen 1.22). God's blessing invoked increase and fruitfulness on what God had already made. In other words the blessing anticipated multiplication and reproduction of the good thing, i.e. life, that God had created. God creates life and then sustains it through his word of blessing.

On the sixth and final day of the Creation project, God creates land animals (livestock, creeping things and beasts of the earth) before his final creative act of making humanity (male and female) in God's image. God then spoke another blessing, this time to the humans saying 'be fruitful and increase in number; fill the earth and subdue it'. In both instances this blessing was intended to create a further increase of the abundant and fruitful *life* that God had made. This is the inherent nature of God's abundance and generosity, that God would bless the creation with the ability to continue to increase. From God's abundance life comes forth, and from these blessings life abounds.

The Psalmist picks up on this idea of blessing in Ps 144.

May our sons in their youth be like plants full grown,

our daughters like corner pillars cut for the structure of a palace;

may our granaries be full, providing all kinds of produce; may our sheep bring forth thousands and ten thousands in our fields;

may our cattle be heavy with young, suffering no mishap or failure in bearing; may there be no cry of distress in our streets!

Blessed are the people to whom such blessings fall!

Blessed are the people whose God is the LORD! (Psalm 144:12–15 ESV)

The blessings are described as youth being like full grown plants, daughters being like the main supporting pillars in a building; full grainstores, healthy pregnant sheep and cattle and a lack of distress in both the fields and the streets. This is the picture of God's abundance and provision and it is assumed that the people whose God is the LORD are blessed in such manner.

The gift of 'God as Father'

Continuing throughout the Old Testament, Israel's God is portrayed as Father to the Hebrew people in the sense of being the one who brings them forth and gives them their identity.

God refers to Israel as 'my firstborn son' (Exodus 4.22) and tells of his love for 'Israel my child' (Hosea 11.1). By taking Israel as a son, God *gives himself as a Father* to Israel. The role of 'son' describes a person's identity in relationship to another person, i.e. with their Father (or mother). In other words, Israel (the people) have been given their unique identity precisely because their Creator God *has given himself to them as their Father*.

The Apostle Paul also picks up on this theme in his letter to the Ephesians. He writes,

"For this reason I bow my knees before the Father, from whom every family in heaven and on earth is named" (Eph 3.14–15 ESV)

Paul understands this connection between creator and father. In Hebrew thinking, to name something is to define it and give it meaning. Remember when God gave Adam the task of naming the animals? That's why names are so important in Scripture often defining the broader situation or destiny of an individual or place. That every family on earth has derived it's *name* from the Father is saying that God, as Creator, has given definition and meaning to humanity.

Many in the contemporary church have discovered the wonderful intimacy of knowing God as their heavenly Father, myself included, but there is flip side of the coin that many of these same believers are slower to embrace. In eastern (hebraic) thinking, a Father also carries authority over the family. I understand that in our modern world the idea of patriarchy has many unsettling connotations attached to it, but the Bible is not a modern book. It is an ancient book set in an ancient world and we must connect to it's ancient worldview to better understand what it might say to us today.

Our loving heavenly Father, is also a Father who possesses authority and power and requires humble obedience from his children. It is here that our own tainted and distorted views of words like 'obedience' and 'authority' can cloud our understanding. The Father loves extravagantly, but nonetheless asks for humble obedience from his children. We cannot choose one of these over the other. They come together.

There is a famous photo of the young John Kennedy Jr. playing happily under the Resolute Desk in the Oval office of the White House in 1963, while his father goes about his presidential business. His father, John F Kennedy, then President of the United States of America, was arguably the most powerful man on the planet... but John Jr got to call him "Dad". I offer this as a somewhat poor analogy of our intimate relationship to our Heavenly Father, but nonetheless a reminder that our loving Father is also the all-powerful Creator.

The gift of God through covenant

This relationship between God and His people is defined through something called a *covenant*.

In those ancient days, covenants were a common way of creating alliances between individuals or tribes. Back then nations did not exist in the way that we think of them today. There was no central government with a border force or constitutional legal system. Instead there were tribes and people groups who exercised dominion over the territories they occupied, whether farming the land or keeping flocks. Covenants were agreements that defined relationships between groups or individuals and they often defined issues around identity, protection and provision. These were matters of utmost importance as they quite literally impacted the chances of survival and longevity of your tribe.

God revealed himself to the Hebrew patriarchs as a God of covenant. In the book of Genesis, God makes covenants with several individuals including Noah and Abram which culminates generations later with God keeping his covenant promises with their Hebrew descendants whom he rescues from their slavery in Egypt. The big picture agreement that he makes with these Hebrew slaves is that "I will take you to be my people, and I will be your God, and you shall know that I am the Lord your God… I am the Lord" (see Ex 6.7). In other words, God invites the Hebrews into a special kind of relationship where they *belong* to each other and share a covenant identity together.

If the description of covenant sounds a little like a marriage, that is because Christian marriage is a form of covenant relationship. The difference is that the marriage covenant is made between two equals, whereas in the divine covenant that God makes with us, God is the greater divine party and humanity is the lesser party. In spite of their full commitment to one another, they cannot offer themselves equally to each other. Humanity is not like God! God gives himself to the Hebrews in covenant relationship, with the intention of inviting many others in to that covenant as well. But it starts with the Hebrews.

When God makes his covenant with Abram in Genesis 12-17, he tells Abram,

> *I will make of you a great nation, and I will bless you and make your name great, so that you will be a blessing. I will bless those who bless you, and him who dishonors you I will curse, and in you all the families of the earth shall be blessed (12.2-3)… to your offspring I will give this land (12.7)…I will make you exceedingly fruitful, and I will make you into nations and kings shall come*

*from you. And I will establish my covenant between me and you
and your offspring after you throughout their generations for an
everlasting covenants, to be God to you and to your offspring
after you. And I will give to you and to your offspring after you
the land of your sojourning, all the land of Canaan, for an everlasting possession, and I will be their God (17.6-8).'*

God is defining the terms of this special covenant relationship with
Abram and his future offspring. It is defined by expressions of God's
generosity toward Abram, his family and his future offspring (which
Mr and Mrs Abram have not yet managed to conceive). Abram's family line will come to be identified by their relationship with God. In
fact, God will come to be identified as 'the God of Abraham, Isaac and
Jacob'. Their relationship defines their covenant *identity*. There will
also be *provision* of a land to live in and a promise of *protection* (God
will curse whoever dishonors Abram). Yet God is so generous that
this blessing is not meant to stop with Abram and his descendants.
God wants *all the families of the earth* to experience this blessing that
begins with Abram. God's blessing is intended to bring increase, multiplication and abundance which in turn can be shared with others
that they too might 'taste and see the Lord is good' (Ps 34:8).

At the very heart of this covenant relationship is God offering
Abram relationship with Himself. *To be in covenant relationship with
God is to receive God's gift of Himself* - a relationship that embraces His
identity, His protection and His provision.

God gave Himself as a gift to Abram in covenant and intended all
the families of the earth to blessed by it. The story of the Old Testament is the story of, among other things, how God's people experienced God's generosity through this special covenant that He made
and kept with them, even when they failed to keep covenant with

God.

In John's gospel we see a *new* covenant described in the opening verses when we read,

> *"[Jesus] came to his own, and his own people did not receive him. But to all who did receive him, who believed in his name, he gave*
>
> *the right to become children of God, who were born, not of blood nor of the will of the flesh nor of the will of man, but of God"* (John 1.11–13 ESV)

In other words, God continues to give himself as a Father by giving the right of sonship to whoever receives his son Jesus Christ. This is a theme that we will keep coming back to.

There is an apocryphal story that illustrates this quite nicely.

> *There once was a fabulously wealthy man who loved his son above all things. To stay close to his son, they began to build an art collection together. Every spare minute, they were out at auctions and sales acquiring rare works of art: everything from Picasso to Raphael. They built one of the rarest most valuable collections in the world. When war broke out, a letter came one day informing the son he had been drafted. The father offered to pull some strings, but the son felt compelled to serve his country as his father and grandfather did before him.*
>
> *The son went off to war, but he wrote his dad everyday. One day the letters stopped. The father's worst fears were realized when he received a telegram from the war department informing him his son had been killed while attempting to rescue another soldier. About six months later, there was a knock at the door. A young soldier with a large package under his arm said, "Sir, you*

don't know me, but I am the man your son saved on that fateful day in battle. He had already saved many lives that day, and as he was carrying me off the battlefield, he was shot through the heart and died instantly.

"Your son was my friend and we spent many a lonely night 'in country' talking about you and your love for art." The young soldier held out his package and said, "I know this isn't much and I'm not much of an artist, but I wanted you to have this painting I've done of your son as I last remember him. The father tore open the package and fought back the tears as he gazed at a portrait of his one and only son. He said, "You have captured the essence of my son's smile in this painting and I will cherish it above all others." The father hung the portrait over his mantle. When visitors came to his home, he always drew attention to the portrait of his son before he showed them any of the other masterpieces.

When the father died the news went out that the entire collection was being offered at an exclusive private auction. Collectors and art experts from around the world gathered for the chance of purchasing one of them. The first painting on the auction block was the soldier's modest rendering of his son. The auctioneer pounded his gavel and asked someone to start the bidding. The sophisticated crowd scoffed and demanded the Van Gogh's and the Rembrandts be brought forth. The auctioneer persisted. "Who will start the bidding? $200? $100?" The crowd continued to turn up their noses, waiting to see the more serious paintings. Still the auctioneer solicited, "The son! The son! Who will take the son? Finally a squeaky voice from the back said, "I'll bid $10 for the son." The bidder was none other than the young soldier the son had died saving. He said, "I didn't come to buy anything and all I have is $10 to my name, but I bid it all." The auctioneer continued seeking a higher bid, but the angry crowd began to chant,

"Sell it to him and let's get on with the auction." The auctioneer pounded the gavel and sold the painting for the bid of $10. An eager buyer from the second row bellowed, "Finally, on with the auction." And just then the auctioneer said, "The auction is now officially closed." The hostile crowd demanded to know how after coming, all this way could the auction possibly be over? The president of the auctioning company came to the microphone and said, "When I was called to conduct this auction, I was told of a stipulation in the will I could not divulge until now. According to the wishes of the deceased only the painting of the son was to be sold today and <u>whoever takes the son gets it all</u>. So today, for $10 this young man has bought one of the world's most priceless art collections and the entire estate in which it is housed -- auction closed." And with the swing of the gavel, the crowd sat in stunned silence staring at the young soldier.[5]

The story serves to illustrate how God gives the richness of this abundant inheritance to those who will receive his Son, Jesus. To accept the gift of the Son is also to receive the Father as a gift.

It is now to the gift of the Son that we turn our attention.

Chapter 3: JESUS IS THE GIFT

"For God so loved the world, that he gave his only Son..."

(John 3:16)

"remember the words of the Lord Jesus, how he himself said, 'It is more blessed to give than to receive." (Acts 20:35 ESV)

I t is December as I sit writing this chapter. I have just ordered some Christmas gifts for my family online and am expecting them to be delivered to me in the next few days. When they arrive, I will hide them away, wrap them (probably on Christmas Eve) and then give them to my family on Christmas Day as is our tradition. I have enjoyed thinking about how to bless them and while I confess I generally hate shopping (and am sorely lacking in gift wrapping skills), it is a joy to give a gift, especially to those I love the most.

The irony of our modern commercialized Christmas is not lost on me. Today we are bombarded by advertising and deals that encourage us to spend, spend, spend on gifts for Christmas. It is a multi-billion dollar business opportunity every year. But do the gifts that we give each other at Christmas find lasting value in our lives? How often do they become unwanted objects that end up being exchanged for 'something you really want'. In other words, we often turn receiving gifts from other people into the activity of buying stuff for ourselves.

And yet many people who participate in this frenzy of Christmas giving (or more cynically, Christmas buying), have no idea that God has already given to them a gift of unfathomable worth that is the real 'reason for the season'. It is a gift that has eternal value. That gift is the person of Jesus Christ, God's own Son.

Some people reject this gift because of the wrapping that it is presented in. This is tragic, because the wrapping is not the gift! Others reject this gift because they have not been told the value or significance of Jesus, hence they deem it to be an unnecessary or irrelevant gift. Others still, have never heard that there is a gift called 'Jesus' that has been freely given to them. They remain blissfully unaware because no-one told them about it and this gift to them goes unclaimed. Nonetheless, the person of Jesus has been given to humanity as God's greatest gift. Jesus is God's gift to us, that comes from God's great love for us.

God gave Jesus as a gift to the world because God loved the world.

God's love language

In Gary Chapman's best selling book entitled 'The Five Love Languages' he lists five differing ways that people commonly communicate 'I love you' to their family and friends. If you are unfamiliar with these love languages, they include spending *quality time* with someone, showing affection through *physical touch*, doing *acts of service* for people, speaking positive *words of affirmation* and lastly, through *giving gifts.*

I always appreciate gifts that people give me. I appreciate that people take the time to think of me and remember me, whether it is on my birthday or at another time. But gift giving actually scores quite low on my list of love languages. For a long time I thought that I was rather immune to hearing 'I love you' through receiving gifts, until a couple of years ago. I realized that while I appreciate people thinking of me when they buy a gift and desiring to show kindness to me, what I crave for is to be known... intimately known.

Not long after my wife and I married, I bought an album recorded by Sir George Martin who was the long time producer for the world famous Beatles. It was one of his final recordings. The CD track list was made up of his personal favorite Beatles tracks which he had recorded with new arrangements performed with a little help from his friends (Beatles pun intended). Anyway, I loved this album and listened to it endlessly. One day I loaned it to a friend... who never returned it.

That was over 20 years ago. I mostly forgot about it. I forgave the friend (I promise), but I missed the music that I loved to listen to. I was sad because for some copyright reason the album was never available on any digital platform, so I couldn't find any way to listen to the album, and having moved from the UK to the USA in the meantime, I never saw the album for sale, in addition to which, CD's have largely gone out of fashion.

Then a couple of years ago for my birthday, my wife gave me the best birthday present I've ever had. With some help from my oldest son and the internet, she had tracked down an original, mint condition CD of the album on eBay and bought it for me for my birthday.

I cried when I opened it.

This gift was so special to me, not because it was expensive (it wasn't... it was actually pretty cheap). It was special because it showed me that my wife *knows* me. She knows my heart. She knows what brings me joy. She was not simply thinking *about* me when she bought it, as nice as that is; the gift demonstrated that she *understands* me; she knows how much I miss this album and understands how much I love the music on it. She values what it means to me. That birthday gift made me feel known and loved and valued. The best gifts do that. They are rare indeed.

When God sent his Son Jesus, he gave us a gift from a place of knowing us intimately as our Creator and knowing what we most needed... restored relationship with God. We need the sense of identity and purpose that comes from connection and belonging. You see God created humanity for relationship and connection with each other but also for relationship and connection with God. Ever since sin entered the world, that connection has been corrupted both between ourselves and between us and God. God the Creator knew that he alone could fully restore the connection that was broken by the first Adam. And so God sent his own Son, the last Adam, as a gift for all humanity. Through Jesus, humanity's connection to our Creator can be restored, and we can be adopted to know him as Father, if we will believe in Jesus, the Son (Jn 1:12).

It is a gift that needs to be received and opened.

In this chapter I want to examine four particular ways in which the Scriptures describe how Jesus has been given as a gift to us. This is not meant to be an exhaustive list, but it is important to ground our understanding in the biblical witness about Jesus. (It is a little theological, but please bear with me).

Let's consider these four expressions of Jesus as God's gift to us:-

i.   Jesus is a ransom payment;

ii.   Jesus is a type of Passover lamb;

iii. Jesus is an atoning sacrifice;

iv.   Jesus came to reveal the Father.

Jesus is a 'ransom for many'

We have considered how God the Father gave his Son to the world as an expression of his love for the world, but Jesus speaks about giving himself on a number of occasions. This self-giving, sacrificial gift, just like the Father, allows Jesus to be both Giver and Gift, Offering and Offer-er, Priest and Sacrifice.

In Matthew 20.28, in the midst of a heated discussion about authority and greatness, Jesus informs his disciples that they must become servants just as he is a servant. He reveals to them that he will give himself 'as a ransom for many'.

> *"Jesus called [his disciples] to him and said, "You know that the rulers of the Gentiles lord it over them, and their great ones exercise authority over them. It shall not be so among you. But whoever would be great among you must be your servant, and whoever would be first among you must be your slave, even as the Son of Man came not to be served but to serve, and to give his life as a ransom for many.""* (Matt 20.25–28 ESV)

When we hear the word ransom, we might be inclined to think of kidnappers demanding payment in return for releasing hostages along with negotiators and armed stand offs. In the context of his day, Jesus is referring to something quite different. The ransom price was the payment that would need to be made in order to purchase the freedom of a person held in slavery (several translations use the word *bond-servant*).

In Jesus culture, very few people were materially wealthy. There was no middle class as we have today. Poverty was widespread. A poor person who could not support themselves through subsistence, might choose to sell themselves into indentured service to work for a master without pay, but in return for food and accommodation. This contractual form of servitude was voluntary, and differed from chattel slavery wherein people were kidnapped or trafficked inhumanely and sold as property. That kind of chattel slavery existed in Jesus day, and sadly still does today, but this form of indentured bond service was a way of coming under the *protection* and *provision* of a Master who had access to greater resources than you (do you recognize these two issues that come into play in forming covenants?). Since, the Master provided for the slave in return for the slave's labor, the only way to be set free from this servitude was to pay the Master a sum of money to cover the loss he would experience by losing the labor of the bond servant. This sum of money was called a *ransom* payment.

Jesus said he had come to give His life as a ransom payment for many people. In other words, his death on the cross would be a self-sacrifice that would have the effect of paying the liberating ransom payment for the many people who needed to be set free from the slavery they lived under. He achieved something that those in slavery could not do for themselves... he paid the *ransom* price to redeem them and set them free. But who or what was the Master that held them in slavery? Jesus tells us in John's Gospel.

> *"Jesus replied, "Very truly I tell you, everyone who sins is a <u>slave to sin</u>. Now a slave has no permanent place in the family, but a son belongs to it forever. So if the Son sets you free, you will be free indeed"* (John 8:34–36 NIV)

So Jesus is saying that SIN is our MASTER because we are SLAVES TO SIN, and slaves don't have a permanent place in the family they serve. Let's just think about this for a moment. As slaves, we are obligated to serve our Master unless we can afford to buy our way out of slavery into freedom, or in other words, pay a *ransom* payment. Well it turns out that none of us can make that ransom payment as slaves to sin. We simply can't afford it. As slaves to sin, we earn the wages of sin. The Apostle Paul tells us that the wages of sin is death (Romans 6.23).

But the Apostle Paul also tells us the good news. "For he has rescued us out of the darkness and gloom of Satan's kingdom and brought us into the Kingdom of his dear Son, *who bought our freedom with his blood* and forgave us all our sins." (Col 1.13–14 TLB)

Again, Paul writes, "It is for freedom that Christ has set us free. Stand firm, then, and do not let yourselves be burdened again by a yoke of slavery." (Galatians 5:1 NIV)

So in his self-giving death, Jesus <u>sets us free</u> from slavery to sin which we could not do for ourselves. What a gift to us!

Some of you reading this may be only too aware of how sin and darkness has had a strong hold on your life. We are not only forgiven for our sins, Jesus has paid the ransom price that enables you to be set free from the hold sin has on you. Because of the cross, God rescues us from a kingdom of darkness and transfers us into the Kingdom of his son Jesus.

In John's Gospel, Jesus refers to himself as a good shepherd who is willing to lay down his life for the sheep under his care. Jesus said, 'For this reason the Father loves me, because I lay down my life that I may take it up again. No-one takes it from me, but I lay it down of my own accord' (John 10.17-18).

Here we see Jesus modeling the sacrificial nature of giving. Jesus laid down his own life willingly of his own accord. This makes the wonder of his death all the more significant.

At the cross, **Jesus life was not taken... it was *given* as a gift,** in order to set us free.

Jesus as a type of 'passover lamb'

The next way that we can understand Jesus as a gift for us is to make the connection back to a major narrative for the Jewish people, which is the story of the Exodus: God's deliverance of the Hebrews from their slavery under Pharaoh in Egypt. The story is told in the book named Exodus. It is worth a little review.

In Genesis 15:13-14, God had previewed with Abram what would unfold for his descendants including predicting their time in bondage in Egypt. The Hebrews found themselves in slavery to the Egyptian Pharaoh for four hundred years, long after the memory of Joseph (the Hebrew prime minister of Egypt) had passed from the collective memory of the Egyptian rulers.

This exodus story of the Hebrew's slavery and subsequent emancipation is also a revealing of the cataclysmic spiritual battle between the idols of the Egyptian pantheon and the Creator God, Yahweh, who has called the Hebrew people to be his own people. As a child, Moses had been saved from infanticide by his quick thinking mother, and in a divine turn of events Moses ended up being raised in the household of the Egyptian Pharaoh, while being nursed by his own mother.

As a young man Moses flees from Egypt and spends forty years as a shepherd in the Midian wilderness (great training for his upcoming assignment!). God meets him at a burning bush, calls Moses to a divine assignment and sends him back to Egypt to lead the Hebrews to their freedom where they will meet with God in the wilderness with Moses as their shepherd leader.

All the while, God is at work hardening the heart of Pharaoh, the Egyptian ruler. Through Moses, the Lord calls the Egyptian tyrant to let the Hebrews go, so that they might be freed from their captivity and go into the desert wilderness to meet with Yahweh and worship him. Pharaoh vacillates in response to Moses requests which leads to God releasing a series of ten plagues against Egypt. Scholars suggest that each plague represents the dethroning of a particular Egyptian god or idol.

The tenth and final plague is to be the most devastating for the Egyptians, and is aimed at destroying all the first born males in Egypt, both human and cattle. This is an attack on the fertility gods of Egypt and hence threatens the very existence of the Egyptians. It also represents an attack on the deification of Pharaoh (himself the first-born son of the previous pharaoh) and casts a major shadow over his ability to protect the Egyptians, in light of the humiliation that the plagues bring to the reputation of the other Egyptian gods.

As the final plague draws close, Yahweh instructs the Israelites to kill and eat a lamb on the eve of this death plague and to daub the lamb's blood onto their doorposts as a sign to them that God will 'pass over' their houses and destruction will not touch them.

"Tell the whole community of Israel that on the tenth day of this month each man is to take a lamb for his family, one for each household ... Take care of them until the fourteenth day of the month, when all the members of the community of Israel must

slaughter them at twilight. Then they are to take some of the blood and put it on the sides and tops of the door frames of the houses

where they eat the lambs. That same night they are to eat the meat roasted over the fire, along with bitter herbs, and bread made without yeast ... On that same night I will pass through Egypt and strike down every firstborn of both people and animals, and I

will bring judgment on all the gods of Egypt. I am the LORD. The blood will be a sign for you on the houses where you are, and

when I see the blood, I will pass over you. No destructive plague
will touch you when I strike Egypt" (Exod 12.3, 6-8, 12–13 NIV)

Notice that the blood on the door post is not a sign for God rather it is a sign for the Hebrews. It signifies that they are being distinguished from the Egyptians as God's people. The blood of the Passover lamb is the identifying mark for the people of God and protects them from the curse of this plague of death. As a result of this 'passing over', the Hebrews are spared from this final fatal plague and are able to make their hasty escape from Egypt into the wilderness to meet with God who will establish his covenant with them.

For these Hebrews, the first Passover is the story of God rescuing them from death and delivering them from the bondage of slavery so that they might meet with God to worship him and enter into the covenant relationship he had promised as Abraham's descendants.

What does this all have to do with Jesus?

Well, Jesus crucifixion happened during the Passover festival. Three of the four gospels describe the last Supper that Jesus shared with his disciples as being the shared commemorative (*seder*) meal of Passover. (Mt 26.17-19; Mark 14.12-17; Luke 22.7-15). This would have been the night before Jesus crucifixion. The Jewish people would be commemorating the original Passover as instructed by God. For the Jews, the *seder* meal is not just a way of recalling the story of what God did on the first Passover simply as history, but it is also a way of *appropriating* God's salvation and deliverance *afresh* in the present moment for those gathered around the seder table.

It is at this seder supper that Jesus institutes a <u>new</u> covenant with his disciples. Author Fleming Rutledge writes,[6]

'the Passover and the exodus are reflected in the Lord's supper in *a number of ways, all of which underscore the active presence of God doing something completely new, even as the ancient saving event is recalled as the prototype. The something-completely-new is that this time, instead of intervening from on high as in the exodus, the intervention has taken place from within God's own life, in the form of the Son's self-offering.'*

During the meal when it came to the traditional moment of breaking of bread, Jesus offers his body for them, 'this is my body, which is given for you'. Then at the set moment in the dinner while drinking the cup of wine he reveals the cup is actually the new covenant in his blood, 'this cup that is poured out for you is the new covenant in my blood' (Luke 22.19-20). While recalling what God did back then, Jesus does something new in that moment together.

On the Cross, Jesus also becomes the first born son who receives into his body the cursed death that comes to those who set themselves in rebellion against God (i.e. Egypt & Pharaoh), thus saving Israel, who is also called God's firstborn son (Exodus 4.22). Jesus stands in that identity to become cursed and so a new Exodus is unleashed rescuing God's people from death and setting them free from the bondage of slavery.

For some reason John's Gospel differs by placing the timing of the last supper on the day before Passover. Therefore Jesus death would have been on the day of preparation of the Passover itself (c.f. John 19.14). This creates a powerful image of Christ being killed at the same time as the lambs were being slaughtered in readiness for the Seder meal. It is Christ's own blood that will become the mark over God's people in accordance with the New Covenant that he established during the Last Supper. It is his blood that now gives us our new identity, and keeps us from the finality of death that sin would bring to us.

The Apostle Paul understood this when he writes to the Corinthians, "for Christ, our Passover lamb, has been sacrificed" (1 Cor 5.7 NIV).

Bishop N.T. Wright offer this perspective:-

> *When Jews of Paul's day kept the Passover festival, they sacrificed lambs in the Temple, continuing the tradition and keeping fresh the memory of God's great deliverance. The early Christians saw Jesus' own death as the climax, the culmination, of this whole tradition. He was the real Passover lamb, and his death had won deliverance for the whole world. The whole Christian life, from this point of view, becomes one long Passover-celebration! That's what it's all about.[7]*

Jesus is a gift to us because in the Lord's Supper and at the cross he presents to us a new Passover. Christ himself becomes the new Passover lamb being slaughtered for the protection and deliverance from death of those entering into a new covenant with him through his blood. His life gives us protection from death and deliverance from bondage.

Jesus is an atoning sacrifice

Have you ever received a gift that when you opened it you looked at it and thought 'what is it' and 'why would I need one of those'? To our modern sensibilities, 'atoning sacrifice' fits into that category of gift. We have to face up to the reality that the world of temples and animal sacrifices is alien to the majority of us in the modern developed world.

While traditions surrounding temples, shrines, candle lighting and prayers remain common throughout many religious communities around the world, the practice of sacrificing animals (or burning grain) remains mysterious to most of us. It is the stuff of folklore, or worse, dark satanic horror stories.

To many people the bible can seemingly be about an ancient and unfamiliar world and yet as Christians we hold that it is the unfolding story of God revealing himself to people throughout history, however distant it may seem from our own time and culture.

This idea of atoning sacrifices is set out in splendid detail in the book of Leviticus, which is not exactly the most widely read book of the bible, precisely because it can seem difficult to make sense of it in our modern world. Some sections of it read more like a butchers manual than a helpful guide to living. And yet it was inspired by God and it was included in the canon of scripture by the early church, because of it's esteemed place in the Jewish Pentateuch/Torah - the first five books of the bible. (I did hear a story once about a butcher who read the book of Leviticus and gave his life to Christ, because he was so enamored by the details of the animal sacrifices, they convinced him that God was interested in him as a butcher... go figure!)

The issue at stake in the first few chapters of Leviticus is that sin, whether it is defined as willful disobedience, accidental rule-breaking or ritual uncleanness, has the effect of disrupting the relations between God and the people he called out of Egypt. Therefore (and forgive me, but I'm going to use some technical words) *expiation* or *propitiation* or *atonement*[8] of sin must be made in order to restore this disrupted relationship. Whatever or whoever is unclean or sinful requires *atonement* since they cannot remain before a holy God without the threat of his judgment. This may not be a popular message today but it is part of how we are to understand God.

The good news in the book of Leviticus is that God, being merciful and kind, provides a means of dealing with this sin and uncleanness, through prescribing these various sacrifices and offerings for the people of God to bring. You can find some examples in Leviticus 1.4, 4.20 & 15:28. Since it was God who invited the people into this special relationship in the first place, it seems only sensible that he would ensure there was a way that this relationship could work. God actually wants this relationship to work but God remains holy in his very nature.

People would bring the relevant offering 'ingredients' to the priests. It may be a bird or a goat or a ram. If they were very poor they could bring a portion of fine flour; it all depended on the specific nature of their involvement with sin. It was the job of the priests to routinely offer these sacrifices at their portable temple (which was a tent or *tabernacle*).   Interestingly, the descriptions of atonement for sins recorded in Leviticus are often accompanied by the declaration 'and they will be forgiven' (e.g. Lev 5.16, 5.18, 6.7), so atonement and forgiveness are connected somehow. The sacrifice didn't let people off the hook for long as this was an ongoing requirement to atone for peoples sin. Perhaps the cost of these sacrifices for a people wandering around a desert wilderness was also meant to be somewhat of a deterrent against repeated sins? If so, it obviously didn't work.

Every year there was a special offering, an atoning sacrifice, made on behalf of all the people in the community. This would require a bull to be sacrificed in a certain way on the Day of Atonement (see Exodus 30:10) and this was carried out by the High Priest. Being a priest was clearly not for the squeamish. In spite of the regular offerings for atonement of the sins of individuals, it was necessary for this special annual offering to be made to atone for the sins of the whole community. This was indeed a holy day and remains so for Jews to-day (though they no longer take animal sacrifices to a temple).

Let's now look at how the New Testament writers connect this to Jesus.

In the book of Romans, Paul writes *"God presented Christ as a sacrifice of atonement, through the shedding of his blood*—to be received by faith. He did this to demonstrate his righteousness, because in his forbearance he had left the sins committed beforehand unpunished" (Rom 3.25 NIV *italics added for emphasis*).

In this verse Paul is saying that once again God provided the means of atonement for sins in order to restore relationship with the people. This time God did it by providing Jesus as the atoning sacrifice. Jesus IS the sacrifice that expiates the disruption of our relationship with God caused by our sins, and therefore this atonement restores the relationship that was previously disrupted. God gives Jesus as a gift to us in this manner. That's good news!

In the book of Hebrews, we read,

> *"for this reason [Jesus] had to be made like them, fully human in every way, in order that he might become a merciful and faithful high priest in service to God, and that he might make atonement for the sins of the people."* (Heb 2.17 NIV).

The author of Hebrews says that Jesus became a merciful and faithful high priest in service to God so that he might make atonement for the sins of the people. In other words, Jesus is both the high priest that offers the atoning sacrifice AND the atoning sacrifice itself… Jesus is offerer and offering; the priest and the sacrifice.

The best news is that Jesus self sacrifice has no expiration date.

> *"Unlike the other high priests, [Christ] does not need to offer sac-*

rifices day after day, first for his own sins, and then for the sins of the people. **He sacrificed for their sins once for all when he offered himself** *"* (Heb 7.27 NIV)

The whole of the Epistle to the Hebrews is one long study in how Jesus fulfilled the role of High Priest and as the atoning sacrifice. It is quite the read, and it is rooted in the sacrifices and offerings described in the book of Leviticus.

As the atoning sacrifice, **Jesus is God's love gift to us**, restoring to us our relationship with God that sin had disrupted.

> *"This is love: not that we loved God, but that he loved us and sent his Son as an atoning sacrifice for our sins."* (1 John 4.10 NIV)

Jesus reveals God

God made us for relationship. We have considered how Jesus restores our disrupted relationship with God by giving himself as an atoning sacrifice. But what kind of God are we being restored to? What is God like?

Jesus is a gift to us because he reveals to us what God is like.

The author of the epistle to the Hebrews writes,

> *"In the past God spoke to our ancestors through the prophets at many times and in various ways, but* **in these last days he has spoken to us by his Son,** *whom he appointed heir of all things, and through whom also he made the universe.* **The Son is the radiance of God's glory and the exact representation of his being,** *sustaining all things by his powerful word."* (Heb 1.1–3 NIV).

Jesus is the *exact representation* of God's being. Another translation says he is the *exact imprint* of God's nature. We get our word English word 'character' from the greek word used here. Jesus reveals God's character.

Elsewhere the Apostle Paul writes, "The Son is the image of the invisible God... for God was pleased to have all his fullness dwell in him" (Col 1.15, 19 NIV). In other words Jesus faithfully reveals to us what God is like, since he is a visible image of the unseen God and the fullness of God's abundance indwells Christ.

One of God's attributes is that God is spirit and that God is *not* like us (c.f. John 4.24, Ps 89.8); how can we know a spirit who is not like us? If we want to know God, then we must look to Jesus.

When Jesus spoke with his own disciples of God being his father, they questioned him about how they could know God. Jesus said,

> *"I am the way and the truth and the life. No one comes to the Father except through me. If you really know me, you will know my Father as well. From now on, you do know him and have seen him." Philip said, "Lord, show us the Father and that will be enough for us." Jesus answered: "Don't you know me, Philip, even after I have been among you such a long time? Anyone who has seen me has seen the Father."* (John 14.6–9 NIV)

In this stunning declaration Jesus tells Philip that the transcendent God has been made known in the incarnate person of Christ. To put it another way God, who is not limited by the constraints of the universe, is revealed within the constraints of creation in the person of Jesus. Not only that but Jesus is saying that God the Father can be known through him. Jesus is the way that we come to know God the Father. It is Jesus intention that we can know God as father for ourselves. In fact this is one of the greatest blessings of the Christian gospel.

Jesus also taught his disciples about the character of God. He used parables and stories to reveal what God is like. Perhaps one of the most famous parables is found in Luke 15. It is the story of a man with two sons. The younger of the two sons asks his father to give him his inheritance early. In the middle eastern culture of the day this was like wishing the father was dead[9]. The boy makes off with his inherited wealth and squanders it on reckless living. Eventually the young man finds himself broke and starving and comes to his senses. He decides to return home and to humbly ask his father if he can work for him as a servant, since he knows he has not fulfilled the expectations of being a good son. The father welcomes home his youngest son with an extravagant display of compassion. In the story the father figure represents God and demonstrates the mercy, compassion, forgiveness and generosity that God shows to those who humbly come to him. Many wonderful books have been written unpacking the wonder of God's character that is on display in this one parable.

In the same chapter of Luke there is another story in which God is described as being like a shepherd who will leave his large flock of sheep behind to search for just one lost sheep, and yet another story where God is described as being like a woman who searches for one lost coin from her collection of coins. God actively looks for lost things and celebrates wildly when he finds them.

Throughout these stories that Jesus told his followers we can see God being revealed. That is one of the reasons why it is so important the Gospels are read and declared and preached in our churches because in them we discover Jesus revealing the truth about God. This is truly good news to those with ears to hear.

In one of his final recorded prayers, Jesus prays,

> "Righteous Father, though the world does not know you, I know you, and they know that you have sent me. **I have made you known to them, and will continue to make you known** in order that the love you have for me may be in them and that I myself may be in them."" (John 17.25–26 NIV)

Jesus came to make God known, to reveal the truth about God the creator to the world that he created.

> Prayer enlarges the heart until it is capable of containing God's gift of himself. (Mother Teresa)

Through Christ, the invisible is made visible, the transcendent becomes immanent, the unknowable becomes knowable and the ineffable God is expressed through the Living Word.

Jesus is a gift to us because through him God is revealed and we are invited into a restored relationship with God as our Father.

Chapter 4: HOLY SPIRIT IS THE GIFT

"If you then, who are evil, know how to give good gifts to your children, how much more will the heavenly Father give the Holy Spirit to those who ask him!"' (Luke 11:13 ESV)

"'Do not leave Jerusalem, but wait for the gift my Father promised, which you have heard me speak about.For John baptized with water, but in a few days you will be baptized with the Holy Spirit.'" (Acts 1.4–5 NIV)

Broken promises can be devastating.

Whether it is the devastation experienced in marriages when the sacred vows are broken, or the pain of a child experiencing repeated broken promises from an absent or abusive parent, the disappointment that stems from an unkept promise can be crushing. So often this disappointment can reframe a persons whole outlook on life allowing doubt and mistrust to take a foothold in even the most trusted relationships.

A common thread through the Old Testament story is that God keeps his promises to his people, while his people continually break their promises to God. God's faithfulness to his word (his promise) is part of his unchanging character that makes him worthy of our trust. Trustworthiness should also be a character trait that marks those who claim his name. To be a people of the Word requires us to be a people of <u>our</u> word; to be promise keepers. Not to do so is to mis-represent God and take his name in vain.

In Acts 2, at the birth of the church, during the Jewish festival known as Pentecost, the apostle Peter delivered his first public sermon to a crowd of festival goers who are perplexed at the scene before them. The Jewish pilgrims have come from every corner of the Roman Empire (hence the list of place names in Acts 2.9-11). They witness a small group of Galileans stumble out onto the streets around breakfast time babbling in a variety of languages and dialects from all around the Mediterranean lands that formed the Roman empire. From their erratic demeanor this small group of disciples are mistakenly presumed to be drunk, yet the perplexed Pentecost pilgrims observing them understand the strange babbling speech as their various regional languages, telling them all about God's mighty works.

According to the biblical account, Peter takes the opportunity to offer an explanation to this eclectic crowd as to what is happening. He begins and ends his sermon talking about the Spirit of God. He systematically unpacks several Old Testament scriptures that provide meaning to what is happening in front of them and also offer an understanding of the significance of the death of Jesus of Nazareth just a few weeks prior.

Peter starts with a quote from the book of Joel.   "And in the last days it shall be", God declares, "that I will pour out my Spirit on all flesh" (Acts 2.17) going on to say,

> *"This Jesus, God raised up, and of that we all are witnesses. Being therefore exalted at the right hand of God, and having received from the Father **the promise of the Holy Spirit**, he has poured*

out this that you yourselves are seeing and hearing." (Acts 2.32–
33).

Finally, Peter calls his listeners to receive God's offer of forgiveness of
their sins by repenting and being baptized. In response to this act of
humility before God, Peter tells them that they "will receive *the gift of
the Holy Spirit... for this promise is for you and for your children and
for everyone who is far off"* (Acts 2.38).

In his sermon Peter reveals the plan of the triune Godhead working
in unity to give Holy Spirit to those who repent and are baptized.
Baptism is the indication of their trust in God. God the Father makes a
promise to give the Holy Spirit to Jesus, which he fulfills at his baptism. This enables Jesus to make the promise to the disciples (in Luke
24.49) that they too must wait to receive this gift of Holy Spirit that
comes from the Father through Jesus. What is happening among the
disciples at Pentecost, according to Peter, is now the outpouring of
this promised gift of the Holy Spirit from the Father through Jesus.

In pouring out the Holy Spirit, God is keeping his promise. He is
fulfilling his word; once again, he is demonstrating his faithfulness.

That the Holy Spirit is the promised gift from God the Father is also
reinforced by Jesus in John's gospel.

> *"And I will ask the Father, and he will give you another Helper, to
> be with you forever, even the Spirit of truth, whom the world
> cannot receive, because it neither sees him nor knows him"* (John
> 14:16–17 ESV)

Though the disciples struggled to understand Jesus meaning at the
time, Jesus was explaining that he must return to the Father and it
was to their advantage that he should go because the Father promised
to send the Helper (Holy Spirit) in his place who would then remain

with them forever. Though Jesus time with his disciples was limited, God's gift to them of Holy Spirit did not have an expiry date.

The Apostle Paul writes years later to the Gentile church in Galatia, rehearsing with them the Gospel to which they had responded. "[God] redeemed us in order that the blessing given to Abraham might come to the Gentiles through Christ Jesus, so that by faith we might receive *the promise of the Spirit*" (Gal 3.14 NIV).

God's faithfulness is so closely woven into his generosity, that it becomes a point of confidence in our relationship with God.

Jesus told a crowd one time, 'if earthly fathers, though evil, know how to give good gifts to their children, how much more can we depend on our Heavenly Father to give the gift of the Holy Spirit to those who ask him'. We expect earthly father to provide for their children, even to acquiesce to their childlike desires at times, simply because of love. Though the best earthly fathers still fall short of perfection, even below average fathers have an innate understanding that they *ought* to provide for their children. Earthly fathers have limited resources and are prone to failing, but through Christ we discover a heavenly Father who is neither limited by resources nor prone to unfaithfulness. It is the Father's good pleasure to give us His Kingdom.

Jesus re-assured his disciples that whatever they ask for in his name, he would do (Jn 14.13). Of course, it is vital to ask 'in his name', in other words, asking on behalf of Jesus in accordance with his character.

A friend of mine regularly uses the analogy of a national ambassador to whom has been delegated great responsibility and influence. When dealing with other nations, the ambassador does not give her opinion or her good ideas. She only re-presents the views and the interests of the nation that has sent her. Likewise when we pray in the name of Jesus, we are not praying our own opinions or good ideas, but are led to pray with the views and interests of the King we represent.

Many years ago, I participated in a student bible study as a university undergraduate. The group mostly consisted of Christians from varying church backgrounds, but often included those who did not yet identify themselves as Christians as they sincerely sought out truth for their lives. I remember on one occasion an earnest seeker attended our study on the theme of prayer and upon hearing John 14.13 became giddy at the idea that this verse might justify him asking God for a winning lottery ticket! We had to have a conversation about whether such a request was legitimately representative of how Jesus would pray, after all Jesus did say to ask for anything!

As with much Kingdom thinking, we must hold two things in tension. We are not to pray selfishly, rather we are instructed to pray with the heart of Jesus who laid down his life for others. In contrast, we are not to limit God's generosity or his desire to answer our prayers but to take a risk by asking for 'anything'. I'm not sure which is worse... to ask in prayer with a naive selfishness or to not ask God because we don't believe that his generosity could extend to giving us 'anything'. The apostle James captures this very thought. 'You do not have because you do not ask. You ask and do not receive, because you ask wrongly, to spend it on your passions' (James 4.2-3). James evidently knew how to hold these two things in tension.

Such can be our confidence in God's generosity, that it is not dependent on what kind of mood God is in, as if God were unstable. Rather our confidence is rooted in the unchanging nature of God (remember *chutzpah* in chapter 1?)

The Holy Spirit is God giving God's self as a gift; a gift that had been promised long before and one that confirms the veracity of God's trustworthiness.

The Apostle Paul also picks up on this idea of the Holy Spirit being a promised gift. In the majestic opening chapter of his letter to the Ephesians, Paul writes about God's delight in choosing to adopt us in Jesus Christ. He then goes on to describe the inheritance that we have obtained because of our adoption by God, before writing,

> 'in him you also, when you heard the word of truth [i.e. God's promise], the gospel of your salvation, and believed in him, you were sealed **with the promised Holy Spirit**, who is **the guarantee of our inheritance** until we acquire possession of it, to the praise of his glory'. Eph 1.13-14 ESV

In other words the Holy Spirit is like the downpayment on a house sale that acts as a guarantee that the transfer of ownership of the house has been secured. In this case however, the promised Holy Spirit is the deposit that guarantees our inheritance as adopted children in God's family, an inheritance to which we are fellow heirs with Christ (Romans 8.16-17). The gift of the promised Holy Spirit gives us confidence for all that God has promised to do.

Let's summarize the three specific ways in which the Holy Spirit is a gift to us, based on some of the Scriptures I have already referred to.

The Spirit of Truth

Jesus refers to the promised Holy Spirit as the spirit of truth, which is a name he gives to Holy Spirit three times in John's gospel (Jn 14.17; 15.26; 16.13). In these verses we learn that the Spirit of truth:

1. Is not accepted by the world, but lives with us and in us (Jn
    14.17). The indwelling of the Spirit of truth distinguishes the
    believer from the world.

2. Goes out (proceeds) from the Father and testifies about Jesus
    (Jn 15.26). The spirit of truth is a distinct person from the Fa-
    ther and Jesus. The Holy Spirit is not Jesus appearing in a dif-
    ferent form. That is the heresy of modalism[10]. God is 'three in
    one', not 'one appearing in three modes'.

3. Will guide us into all truth, speaking only what he hears (Jn
    16.13). The spirit of truth brings the revelation of truth to us
    from the Father, since the Holy Spirit only speaks what the
    Fathers says. The truth is what sets us free.

There is some profound theology in these few verses. Suffice to say,
we must remain faithful to the biblical witness concerning the Holy
Spirit.

Our Comforter & Advocate

The KJV translates John 14.16 as 'he shall give you another com-
forter', while most modern translations either use the word 'advocate',
'helper' or 'counselor'. The greek word is multi-faceted, which is why,
I suppose, the english translations offer so many different words to
translate it. Certainly God is a present source of comfort to those in
distress (we read about that in Paul's opening verses in 2 Corinthians
1). As NT Wright points out, the person who provides comfort to the
troubled offers strength and encouragement in the moment of need,
but does not materially change the circumstances that the sufferer is
facing. The comfort changes us, strengthening us and giving us the

power to continue on in the face of challenge, tragedy or hardship.

However, the word advocate (or counselor) offers a slightly different picture. The word is part of courtroom vocabulary, implying that the Spirit pleads on behalf of us to remind God to move in our favor. As in a courtroom, the advocate ensures that we are not forgotten, and that our situation is represented before the heavenly court, where God is the residing judge. This would explain why Paul describes the Spirit as *'interceding for us with groans too deep for words'* in Romans 8.26. The Holy Spirit is constantly bringing us before the Father in intercession.

We can rejoice knowing the Holy Spirit does not forget us, and is given as a source of comfort to us.

The Spirit of Adoption

In the letter to the Romans, Paul refers to the Holy Spirit as the *spirit of adoption*; "but you have received the Spirit of adoption as sons, by whom we cry, "Abba! Father!" (Rom 8.15 ESV). Again, in his letter to the Galatians he makes the connection between Holy Spirit and our spiritual adoption; "so that we might receive adoption as sons. And because you are sons, God has sent the Spirit of his Son into our hearts, crying, "Abba! Father!"" (Gal 4.5–6 ESV)

It is by this spirit that we are enabled to cry out 'Abba Father' as we awe in our adoptive identity in Christ. Not only does the Spirit make our adoption into God's family a reality to us, but the Spirit is also the downpayment that guarantees our new inheritance as fellow heirs with Christ.

The late New Testament Theologian James G Dunn identifies the significance of this *doctrine of adoption* in his work[11]. "The fact that Paul makes such a similar reference in letters to two different churches (only one of which he knew personally) is a clear enough indication that the sense of sonship, both experienced in and expressed through the 'Abba' prayer, was common in most churches of the diaspora."

Theologian J I Packer calls the doctrine of adoption the 'highest blessing of the gospel[12]'. He also writes,

> If you want to judge how well a person understands Christianity, find out how much he makes of the thought of being God's child, and having God as his Father. If this is not the thought that prompts and controls his worship and prayers and his whole outlook on life, it means that he does not understand Christianity very well at all. For everything that Christ taught, everything that makes the New Testament new is summed up in the knowledge of the Fatherhood of God. 'Father' is the Christian name for God[13].

In my own life this revelation did not become real to me for nearly two decades of following Christ. By Packer's measure, it seems I did not understand Christianity very well at all! In true evangelical fashion I centered my faith on the person of Jesus Christ. I believed in God the Father and God the Holy Spirit doctrinally, and would describe myself as filled with the Spirit, even demonstrating spiritual gifts. In the spring of 2008 during a brief time of worship I encountered the Holy Spirit as the spirit of adoption for the first time. It was both life changing and overwhelming. I received into the very core of my being the revelation that enabled me to cry out 'Abba Father', certain of my adopted status before God and secure in my heavenly Father's love for me. While it was a very emotional experience (I wept for hours), it was not primarily about my emotions. It was about the revelation of my adoption, presented to me by Holy Spirit who is the spirit of truth. My emotions were simply my response to the wonder of this revelation. God has chosen to adopt me and he took pleasure in doing so!

> "Long, long ago he decided to adopt us into his family through Jesus Christ. (What pleasure he took in planning this!)" (Eph 1.5 MESSAGE)

I sort of joke that this was like being 'born again-again'. The effect on my spiritual life was profound. My communion with God was suddenly more intimate, my desire for God was greater, and my spiritual authority as a believer increased significantly. I was a transformed man. My wife saw it, my kids saw it and my church saw it.

This is the beauty of our three in one God. The Father sends the Son and promises the gift of Holy Spirit. Jesus, the son, receives the promise of Holy Spirit, and in giving himself for us, enables us to receive the gift of Holy Spirit. Holy Spirit works in us revealing the Father to us, reminding the Father about us, and realizing our Fathers delight in adopting us.

The Father sends the Son; the Son reveals the Father and sends the Spirit; and the Spirit confirms our adoption by the Father and his love for us.

God giving Gods-self to us is the greatest gift we can receive!

PART TWO: *THE GIFTS FROM THE GIVER*

"The heart of the Giver makes the gift dear and precious"

Martin Luther (1483-1546)

Chapter 5: GIFTS FROM THE FATHER

'If you then, who are evil, know how to give good gifts to your children, how much more will your Father who is in heaven give good gifts to those who ask him!' Jesus, Sermon on the Mount, Matthew 7:11

Each one has a place in the community of Christ, and ought to fill it, but he ought not to be everywhere and want to take part in everything . . . Take note of what God gives you, then you will also know the task he sets you. (Heinrich Emil Brunner[14])

God wants to give good gifts to those who ask him since he is a loving Father. As a parent myself, when I give gifts to my children, I want them to enjoy the gift and take pleasure from it but I also want them to know that it is given as an overflow of my love for them. The two things are connected. Gifts do not replace relationship. Gifts belong in the context of relationship.

The 'grace' gifts from God (Romans 12)

It is always wise to examine the context within which we read any particular verse or passage of Scripture, lest violence be done to its original intent. In the epistle to the Romans, we have Paul writing to the saints in Rome who are loved by God. He writes with great affection and an eager desire to be reunited with his readers. Prior to chapter twelve Paul writes at length regarding the message of salvation and how both the Gentiles and Israel fit into God's broader plan. Neither Israelite nor Gentile earned their salvation or righteousness, but rather God sovereignly chose Israel to bring the message of salvation from God to all nations. Now Gentiles can experience this salvation too because of God's grace that has been poured out through Holy Spirit on both Jew and Gentile. Neither Jew nor Gentile are superior, nor without need of God's mercy. The stage is now set for Paul to appeal to the Roman saints, in light of God's mercy to give themselves fully as living sacrifices to God, not thinking of themselves more highly than they ought to.

> *"For by the grace given me I say to every one of you: Do not think of yourself more highly than you ought, but rather think of yourself with sober judgment, in accordance with the faith God has distributed to each of you. For just as each of us has one body with many members, and these members do not all have the same function, so in Christ we, though many, form one body, and each member belongs to all the others. <u>We have different gifts, according to the grace given to each of us</u>. If your gift is prophesying, then prophesy in accordance with your faith; if it is serving, then serve; if it is teaching, then teach; if it is to encourage, then give encouragement; if it is giving, then give generously; if it is to lead, do it diligently; if it is to show mercy, do it cheerfully." (Romans 12:3–8 <u>NIV</u>)*

So the context for this passage is that the readers should be giving themselves as living sacrifices to God. It makes sense that they should bear this resemblance to the sacrificial, self-giving nature of the God they worship. Hopefully you can start to see why embracing the nature of the Giver will begin to impact your understanding of the gifts.

Paul then unpacks this brief discussion on these gifts of grace. He makes the following noteworthy points:-

     i.   God assigns varying measures of faith to people (Rom 12.3); each of us have been given a measure of faith

     ii.   Just like the members (parts) of one body do not all function the same way, so we (believers) do not all have the same function (Rom 12.4)

     iii.   Individual members have gifts that differ according to the grace given to each member (Rom 12.6) which, by default is a grace that was given to us not earned by us,

     iv.   We are to use the gifts we have been given with the correct motivation (Rom 12.6-8), which is rooted in our call to be a living sacrifice to God, giving of ourselves in the service of others.

The seven grace gifts mentioned here (prophecy, service, the one who teaches, the one who encourages, the one who gives, the one who leads, the one who does acts of mercy) appear to have a specific motivation behind each of them (faith, serving, teaching, exhortation, generosity, diligence, cheerfulness). For this reason, some writers describe this list of gifts as the *motivational* gifts.

The overarching significance of this passage might be expressed this way - Paul is not simply listing what all the gifts are, rather *how* and *why* these particular gifts are to be used. Let's review each in turn.

Prophesying

In this passage, Paul exhorts the one who prophesies to do so according to their faith. Since Paul emphasizes the motivation for each of these gifts it is important that we do not separate prophesying from the measure of faith needed to prophesy.

Prophecy can be defined as 'the gift of interpreting divine will or purpose'.[15] It involves receiving revelation from God and then sharing it with the intended recipient. It can have either a directive sense (forth-telling) or a predictive sense (fore-telling) as well as the obvious revealing sense. Consider 2 Peter 1:21 "For no prophecy was ever produced by the will of man, but men spoke from God as they were carried along by the Holy Spirit."

In church we commonly teach that there are three stages to prophesying. They are *revelation, interpretation & application*. *Revelation* refers to receiving the content of what the Lord shares or reveals to the individual. The content can be words, an impression or a picture or even an action (remember Jeremiah lying on his side). *Interpretation* is the process of decoding and understanding what the revelation actually means. Sometimes this process is very simple as we can receive words whose meaning are plain. However prophetic words can sometimes be highly symbolic and almost like heavenly riddles (c.f. Numbers 12.8). *Application* is the final stage, i.e. knowing how to respond to the prophetic word. Not all prophetic words are predictive in nature. So sometimes, for a promise (rather than a prediction) to be fulfilled it maybe conditional on our response in faith to the word. Often a prophetic word will confirm something that God is doing or saying already, hence encouraging that person and building up their faith that God is at work.

Paul also tells his readers to prophesy in proportion to their faith. In other words, people with little measure of faith are to prophesy in accordance with their little measure of faith. People with great faith are to prophesy according to their great faith. The first time I stood up to share a prophetic word (I forget the setting) it was in proportion to the little amount of faith I had to prophesy at the time. I think it sounded something like, "err... I think the Lord really wants you to know that...err... he really loves you!" You might laugh, you might even question whether telling someone that God loves them constitutes a genuine prophetic word, but in that moment, that was the message that God wanted to share with that particular person that was within my measure of faith to offer. When I prophesy now, my faith is much greater in terms of delivering what I sense God is showing me. I still need to pray for the interpretation and application, and as the one delivering the message I have increasingly discovered that God doesn't always give me those two parts. Often the recipient understands the interpretation and application immediately, even though the revelation may not make much sense to me.

I remember a Sunday morning when the Lord highlighted a particular couple in our church to me during our worship service. I sensed the Lord wanted to encourage them that he was at work in their lives. In my spirit I 'saw' a green apple over the head of the husband. Wanting to be faithful (but also wanting to be encouraging) I shared this with him and told him, I think God is telling you he will make you fruitful (that was me trying to interpret the revelation). The husband chuckled at me, and told me that after searching for a new job he recently took a well paid job with Apple computers. It was simply a confirmation that God had provided this job for him. My interpretation was not harmful, but it was of my own doing. I've learned that I am to simply share the revelation, and see whether the Lord provides the interpretation or application to me or someone else. I just have to be faithful with what I am given.

The Apostle Paul instructed the Thessalonians not to despise prophecy (something that many in the church today would do well to receive) but it is also clear that Paul expected them to test all prophecies[16] (something that many others in the church would do well to receive). The importance of properly testing prophecy cannot be overstated, but is sadly often ignored. Prophecy must stand up to the plumb-line of what God has already spoken and revealed through his Word in the Scriptures and be in line with his character. Again, this is why Part One of this book is so important. God won't speak in contradiction to his nature.

Serving

The word we translate as *service* can also be translated as 'ministry'. We get the word 'deacon' from the same root word. The connotation is that we are carrying out the commands of someone for the benefit of another, in this case *God's* commands for the benefit of his people.

Paul highlights that serving is not just an action but it is also a heart motivation. To be honest, I know that there are times when I have served with a bad attitude. I have done it begrudgingly without honoring the ones I am serving. Paul is saying that when we operate with the gift of serving then it comes with a grace for service.

We recently held our annual volunteer appreciation lunch at our church. Once a year, to show our appreciation for our volunteers, our Pastors serve lunch to our amazing volunteer team, consisting of around two hundred people who freely serve in our church in various capacities, from children's ministry to ushers, car parking directors to language translation, small group leaders to prayer team members. We have a wonderful culture of service in our church. But what makes our volunteers so amazing is the motivation and heart with which they serve. They do it joyfully, wholeheartedly and to the best of their ability.

We teach our new church members that in the New Testament there is no difference between ministry and service. To minister is to serve. To serve is to minister. Just because I am a pastor does not mean I am released from stacking chairs, pouring coffee, using the vacuum cleaner or clearing away after meetings. In fact, I think I am meant to demonstrate service through my leadership all the more. My entire vocation is an act of service to God and to others. When 'ministers' preach or lead worship or preside over communion, their motivation should be to serve others, not to build their own egos. These ministry tasks do not make them superior over those they serve. They may be tasks with a greater level of spiritual responsibility that require increased spiritual sobriety, but they remain an act of service. Ministry is service to God and to others.

One of the most humbling things I have ever been told by certain people over my years as a church pastor is that I have restored their trust in ministers and pastors. It breaks my heart when I hear their stories of how church ministers have abused their ministry positions to hurt and manipulate people. I wish I had only heard this story once or twice but I am shocked at how often I have heard it from a wide variety of people. Jesus spoke very plainly to his disciples on this issue.

"Jesus called [the disciples] together and said, "You know that those who are regarded as rulers of the Gentiles lord it over them, and their high officials exercise authority over them. Not so with you. Instead, whoever wants to become great among you must be your servant, and whoever wants to be first must be slave of all.

For even the Son of Man did not come to be served, but to serve…"" (Mark 10:42–45 <u>NIV</u>)

Jesus himself came in the form of a servant and showed his disciples the example of service that they were to follow when he washed their feet, instructing them to go and do likewise (Phil 2.7; Jn 13:5-14). To exercise the gift of service (ministry) properly, the servant heart of our God must be revealed.

Teaching

The greek word translated as teaching is '*didasko*' from which we get our English word 'didactic'. When we teach we instruct others.

The purpose of teaching is to impart something to others. It is not simply an informational transaction. The purpose of the Jewish rabbi's teaching was to reproduce themselves through their disciples. It is a very western construct to consider information transfer as successful teaching. The Hebraic understanding of teaching is more like apprenticing your disciples. When I teach you then I am giving myself to you through my wisdom and experience as well as through inspired revelation. While it will include information transfer it will be much more than that. That means that when I teach I am investing myself into those who I am teaching. Teachers should study in order to learn, and then share what they have learned. This is a subtle but very important distinction. We can tell people about something we heard or read, but we can only really teach people something that we have actually learned and mastered ourselves.

It may seem obvious to say that if you are gifted to teach, then it is important to pay attention to what you teach. The content that you bring through your teaching matters. In fact, I think that this is at the heart of the motivation that Paul is describing. You should be motivated to teach because of your commitment to the benefit that it brings, not because of some need you have for your voice to be heard or for your opinion on a subject to be validated. Christian teacher's have a commitment to share God's ways and God's truths.

The New Living Translation says "if you are a teacher, teach well". If you have the opportunity to teach then learn to teach well. Teach so that others will learn and reproduce what you are teaching. Great teachers know how to create great learning environments. They are not concerned with appearing clever, but they are concerned about helping others to learn. Not all teachers excel at standing in front of a large room full of people. Some excel through using the medium of writing; others excel in smaller group settings.

One of my primary gifts is teaching. What is really interesting to me is that people started recognizing my gift in very mundane environments. I remember an occasion when I was having lunch with a couple and as I explained something to them they both commented that I had an ability to explain complex things in simple ways. On another occasion in a group exercise at a former workplace I shared with a small group something that I had learned on a training course. Afterwards two people came up to me separately and asked if I had ever considered teaching in a more formal setting.

I have chosen to take every opportunity to develop the gift that I believe God has given me. It is not fully developed yet and I need to continue to steward it well. I also need to continually guard my motivation for teaching, which is to invest in others and see them learn and grow in understanding. Teachers teach for the glory of God and for the benefit of others, not to feel important!

Finally, the one who teaches needs to be submitted to the Holy Spirit who is our teacher and who leads us into all truth (John 14.26; 16.13). We are not seeking human wisdom, but wisdom that comes from above (James 3.17).

Encouraging

The greek word translated as encouragement (or exhortation) literally means 'to come alongside'. The Holy Spirit is referred to using a root of this word in John 14.16 which is often translated as 'Helper'. There is a wonderful gift of encouragement and exhortation that the body desperately needs. This kind of encouragement is not shallow 'cheerleading' from the sidelines telling everybody that they're 'awesome' all the time. Instead this kind of exhortation comes from a steadfast faithfulness to walk alongside people and call them to all that God has for them. Exhortation will usually require us to be present with people in the moment, to truly come alongside them. It is a wonderful pastoral gift.

The one who exhorts literally 'en-courages' someone - enabling them with courage! Whatever their present circumstance might be once they have had an encounter with encouragement and exhortation they should be more courageous and joyful about pressing on. The encourager has not changed the circumstances, but has helped change the perspective of the one facing the challenge to help them see things differently.

An encourager is not simply an advice giver!

Have you ever been given unhelpful advice you didn't ask for and felt like it was given to show off how clever the advisor was? That should never be our motivation. It is interesting that sandwiched either side of this short passage on gifts, Paul is telling the Roman church to not think more highly of themselves than they ought and then to out-do one another in showing honor to others (Rom 12.3 & 10). These are the overwhelming Kingdom values that form the environment for these spiritual gifts to flourish. As with all the gifts, they are given for the benefit of others.

In Acts 4.36, we read about a man called Joseph (better known as Barnabas) whose nickname was 'Son of Encouragement'. Barnabas is the one who mentors the apostle Paul after his conversion eventually enabling Paul to meet with the Jerusalem church leaders that he had previously been persecuting. The newly transformed Paul was highly controversial in the young church given that he had been their chief persecutor. Barnabas stood alongside him, risking his own reputation on Paul and opening doors for him. The Apostle Paul's success in ministry was shaped in no small measure by the Barnabas' ministry of encouragement. Barnabas also played a role in encouraging John Mark who had fallen out with Paul after their first missionary journey (Acts 15.36-41). Barnabas believed in John Mark when Paul wouldn't give him the time of day. John Mark is widely believed to be the author of Mark's gospel having been a companion of both the Apostle Peter and Paul. Barnabas was the one who had the privilege of bringing encouragement and exhortation to both Paul and John Mark, two of the New Testaments most powerful writers, no wonder he got the nickname he did. Where would we be today without the ones who exhort and encourage?

Giving

Have you ever considered that the act of giving is itself a gift? The Greek word used has the connotation of sharing from what you have. Have you ever received a gift at just the right time that was particularly meaningful to you? Paul encourages those who have the gift of giving to do so with generosity and liberality. Once again, the motivation is generosity not self-promotion. There should be no strings attached to our giving. We don't give in order to win brownie points or to store up favor in the future.

Paul does not necessarily have financial giving in mind, though it is certainly not excluded from what he is talking about. He uses exactly the same word at the opening of this same letter, when he tells the saints in Rome that he longs to see them so that he can 'impart' some spiritual gift to strengthen them. He is wanting to share what he has received. I think of Jesus telling his disciples in Matthew 10 that because they have received freely, they should give freely (the greek vocabulary is connected but not exactly the same). In like manner, Paul seems to be encouraging the Roman saints to share what they have received with a generous heart that does not expect something in return.

In his Sermon on the Mount, Jesus warned his listeners of the folly of giving in order to look good in front of other people. Not only can such false displays rob you of receiving your heavenly Father's reward, but it also dishonors the person to whom you are giving. They are simply being used as a pawn in a game of self promotion and are not receiving an authentic demonstration of God's grace.

Paul writes to the church in Corinth inviting them to give to his collection for the Jewish Christians experiencing suffering in Jerusalem.

He tells them not to give out of compulsion or with reluctance but rather with cheerfulness and hilarity, since this it what God loves. After all, we learned in Part One that God is the most generous being we can ever encounter. It makes perfect sense that the manifestation of his gift to us would lead us to radical generosity towards others.

> *A cheerful giver does not count the cost of what he gives. His heart is set on pleasing and cheering him to whom the gift is given.* (Julian of Norwich)[17]

The church that I have served in for the past decade has taught me so much about generosity. Being around leaders who have this gift of giving that flows from a heart of generosity has deeply impacted me. I had so many excellent role models, especially in Che & Sue Ahn our Senior Pastors. As I spent time in this environment I slowly absorbed this value of generosity and giving became a joyful discipline.

After I had been at the church for a couple of years and my sons entered their teen-years, my oldest son said, 'Dad, do you want to know something that I've noticed about you?' Full of trepidation at the thought of my teenage son sharing his honest thoughts about me to my face, I asked him what is was that he had noticed. He replied, 'You've become much more generous!'

After the initial relief subsided (anyone with opinionated teenage children will understand), I became curious as to what it was that he saw change in me. After all, although I *had* learned to be more generous financially to others, I never waved our checkbook in front of my son or told him about financial gifts we had made in secret to others (refer back to Matt 6:2-4). Generosity is manifested in everything from the way we speak to others to the way we act around others, preferring them, honoring them, giving them the benefit of the doubt and being willing to serve them. Generosity goes way beyond money, though it includes it of course. Paul Manwaring says it this way, "The biggest mistake you can make is to think that worship is just about singing or that generosity is just about money". Often, my most precious asset is my time, and I have learned to be much more generous with my time than I was before.

How about being generous with our time, relationships, ideas and homes too?

I pray that in our money-focused western culture God would release more and more selfless, generous and hilarious givers who model God's own heart.

Leading

Leadership is a spiritual gift that God gives. It is not a reward for long service! The Apostle Paul is concerned that those who the Lord has gifted with leadership should carry a motivation of diligence and care in order to lead well. This involves serving others and not thinking more highly of ourselves than we ought. The New Testament use of this word always carries a sense of 'caring for' those being led[18], so it includes the pastoral dimension of a shepherd leader.

In our modern western culture, especially in the business world, we have embraced a kind of 'cult' of leadership. The church sadly, is not immune. Books on leadership abound in every bookstore. I do believe that some skills to being a good leader can be learned by everyone. But Paul is communicating that leading (or ruling) is a grace gift that is given by God.

Christian leadership is not about 'titles' or status. Instead it is about recognizing the responsibility that God has given some to care for and lead others. In other words, within the body of Christ spiritual authority is not given because someone has a job title, but rather a position of leadership is given to recognize the corresponding God-given authority that has been graced to that person. Many churches have a discernment process in order to recognize this grace on an individual and hence release them into positions of responsibility. In other churches, leaders might be appointed on the basis of personality or charisma which, while appealing, are not the same as this grace for leadership.

Paul wants those who lead to do so with an earnest commitment (diligence). Whether we lead our family, a small group or a megachurch we are to lead with this kind of eagerness. It is a reminder that leadership is a gift that serves others (the whole point and context of this passage) and so it should be administered with devotion to those we are leading. This kind of leadership is not self-serving. We don't exercise leadership for the perks of a position! No, remember the main premise here. The gifts reveal the Giver. Leadership reveals the self-sacrificial nature of God.

In 2014, author and management theorist Simon Sinek, presented a TED talk entitled 'Why good leaders make you feel safe'. He identifies from research and interviews that he has collated that great leaders implicitly have a concern and love for the people that they lead. During his talk he makes this comment.

> *You know, in the military, they give medals to people who are willing to sacrifice themselves so that others may gain. In business, we give bonuses to people who are willing to sacrifice others so that we may gain… The closest analogy I can give to what a great leader is, is like being a parent. If you think about what being a great parent is, what do you want? What makes a great par-*

ent? We want to give our child opportunities, education, discipline them when necessary, all so that they can grow up and achieve more than we could for ourselves. Great leaders want exactly the same thing. They want to provide their people opportunity, education, discipline when necessary, build their self-confidence, give them the opportunity to try and fail, all so that they could achieve more than we could ever imagine for ourselves.[19]

This kind of leadership (that makes people feel cared for and valued) is the kind of leadership grace that Paul is referring to here in Romans 12. Paul likens his leadership to the responsibility of being a Father; protecting, caring, training. Again, I refer you back to Jesus model of servant leadership in Mark 10.43. Once again, it is a display of the nature of the Giver of this wonderful gift.

Showing mercy

We have come to the final gift listed in this particular passage; acts of mercy. Acts of mercy are demonstrations of kindness and concern for someone in serious need. It is a reflection of the mercy (steadfast love) that God bestows towards us because he has willingly bound himself to us through his covenant to his people. The Old Testament is full of declarations and demonstration of God's mercy/ faithful kindness/ love shown towards his people. Therefore for Christians there is a subtext that reflects our obligation to those we are now bound to in the name of Christ. Whether it be done to neighbor or stranger (Jesus blurred the lines nicely for us on that), acts of mercy are to be done with cheerfulness and good will, but also from a place of understanding our deep obligation to care for those around us. Mercy is demonstrated well in the parable of the Good Samaritan, who stops to care for the wounded Jewish traveler (Luke 10). The prophet Micah reminded the Israelites, "what does the LORD require of you? To act justly and to love *mercy* and to walk humbly with your God." (Micah 6.8 <u>NIV</u>)

We have largely forgotten the concept of communal obligation in our Western culture, in part because we no longer remember to whom we belong, instead having settled for highly individualistic lifestyles that separate us from our neighbors. Those who are communally minded are often accused of being 'socialist' (a modern atheistic political ideology concerning the method of re-distribution of material possessions), when in reality 'communal care' is a deeply theological and ancient issue rooted in the Judeo-Christian tradition of loving our neighbor and valuing human life created in the image of God. Sadly it often takes major disasters for this sense of community and belonging to become apparent, perhaps because such events help us to realize that none of us are immune from such tragedies because of our perceived status or zip-code.

The same cheerfulness with which Paul exhorts the Corinthians to give to the Jerusalem relief effort is the cheerfulness with which we are to show mercy! We get our English word *hilarious* from the greek root used here. Paul is saying that these acts of mercy shown to the needy and afflicted should be done with a heart of great joy and cheerfulness. I love the idea of bringing joyful mercy to those who need cheering up! Truly this is a re-presentation of the heart of our God.

Wrapping up the Father's gifts

As a reminder, let's remember the context for these gifts in Paul's letter to the Romans.

i.   They are *to foster unity*, not individualistic pride; just as the members of our triune God constantly point to and glorify one another so God's grace is given to the humble,

ii.   they are given *for mutual service* not for self aggrandizement; the gifts in operation always lead to the blessing of others, not to self-indulgence,

iii.   they *are demonstrations of God's grace*, not rewards or badges of honor.

Paul is just as concerned about how the gifts are exercised as he is with listing particular gifts, but above all Paul is concerned that *they should reveal the character of the Giver of grace.*

Chapter 6: GIFTS FROM JESUS

"This is why it says: "When [Christ] ascended on high, he took many captives and gave gifts to his people." (Ephesians 4:8 NIV)

"The gifts he gave were that some would be apostles, some prophets, some evangelists, some pastors and teachers," (Eph-esians 4:11 NRSV)

When I was little my Dad would occasionally travel over-seas for business. Back then we didn't have cell phones or email, so we would rarely hear from him during his trip. Perhaps he would call my Mum to let her know he had landed safely. I don't remember much about how long my Dad was away for, but I do remember that when he arrived home, he always brought back gifts for us. When he traveled to Canada one time he got me a Toronto BlueJays baseball cap and player figurine (I think I still have the cap in a box somewhere). Another time he went to Malta and was able to take my Mum with him. He brought me back a t-shirt with a big logo on the front that said, 'My parents went to Malta, and all I got was this lousy T-shirt!' There were other trips and other gifts, but I still re-member those ones to this day.

After Jesus rose from the dead and had spent some time with his disciples, he returned home to be with his Father in heaven. Because Jesus 'ascended into heaven' we refer to this as the Ascension (read Acts 1). It turns out that when he went home Jesus gave out gifts on his return, a bit like my Dad did after his business trip. We read about this in Ephesians chapter four. However, unlike my Dad, who gave gifts to his family who had stayed at home, Jesus gave gifts to his people that he had left behind when he returned to heaven.

The list of these 'Ascension' gifts in Ephesians 4 was where I first started my journey into discovering how each person of the Trinity give gifts. These gifts are, in my opinion, the most strategic, as well as the most poorly understood gifts that Paul mentions. I intend to deal with this passage and its implications in quite a bit of detail because of its strategic importance for the church today. For consistency let's set some context for Paul's letter to the Ephesians before we examine the 'gifts' themselves.

Location location location

Most scholars believe that Paul's letter was actually a circular letter to the churches across Asia Minor (modern day Turkey - an often overlooked region that continues to be a melting pot of cultural, religious and political ideologies). Unlike Paul's letters to the Corinthian church which were written to a specific community and in response to particular local issues, this letter to the Ephesian churches deals with broader theological issues that all the churches in the region are to be informed of.

Geography is not the only location of importance for this passage. Its location within the letter as a whole also matters. Paul writes broadly on the nature of salvation and the foundations of unity in the Church, but also with regards to the ideal for internal relationships among believers (sometimes referred to as the 'household codes'). At the beginning of chapter four, Paul turns his emphasis to the theme of unity in the body reminding his readers of the one Lord, one baptism and one faith they all share. This unity is attained through humility and in the work of building the bond of peace between one another. It is this specific location within the letter that leads me to believe that the gifts mentioned in Ephesians 4.11 are therefore of great importance to the unity of the church.

But grace was given to each one of us according to the measure of Christ's gift. Therefore it says, "When he ascended on high he led a host of captives, and he gave gifts to men." (In saying, "He ascended," what does it mean but that he had also descended into the lower regions, the earth? He who descended is the one who also ascended far above all the heavens, that he might fill all things.) And he gave the apostles, the prophets, the evangelists, the shepherds and teachers, to equip the saints for the work of ministry, for building up the body of Christ, until we all attain to the unity of the faith and of the knowledge of the Son of God, to mature manhood, to the measure of the stature of the fullness of Christ, so that we may no longer be children, tossed to and fro by the waves and carried about by every wind of doctrine, by human cunning, by craftiness in deceitful schemes. (Eph 4:7-14)

Five graces from Jesus to his church

According to Paul, *each one of us* has received grace from Christ according to the measure of *his* gift, and this is confirmed by the Old Testament Scripture which Paul then quotes, "When he ascended on high he led a host of captives, and he gave gifts to men".[20] Since *each*

of us have received grace from Christ these gifts have been distributed widely among us all and have not been confined to just a few.
This is a major mindset shift that the church needs to lay hold of. This
is not a list of staff positions for professional Christians. This is the call
of each one of us.

When he ascended into heaven Jesus gave out gifts to those in his
Kingdom (i.e. those of us who are now 'slaves to Christ' and citizens
of his kingdom as Paul might say elsewhere). The imagery Paul is
drawing from is that of a conquering Roman general leading his captives before him as a sign of his victory and then generously bestowing gifts from the battle spoils as a sign of his great benevolence. It is
not unlike the triumphal imagery he uses in 2 Corinthians 2:14.

The next thing to note is that we are given a measure (or portion) of
a gift. Different people have different measures. There is no reason to
presume that the measure of 'prophet' is given to each person equally.
Some receive a greater portion than others (in keeping with many of
the parables Jesus told about the Kingdom). Paul is indicating that
there are different degrees of gifting and anointing across the body, to
suit the calling and purpose of each one.

Paul then describes these gifts as 'the apostles, the prophets, the
evangelists, the shepherds and teachers'. So it appears that these grace
gifts are *people*, or perhaps more specifically, people whose function
emulate the ministry of Jesus in some specific way. Think about that.
Rather than giving a merely 'spiritual' gift, Jesus - God incarnate, the
Word who became flesh - gives people as gifts to the church; real life,
embodied people! Their purpose is clear enough. They are given to
equip the saints for the work of ministry (service) so that the whole
body might mature into the full stature of Christ. Once again, these
people-as-gifts are given for the benefit of the whole body of Christ in

order that the body would come to a place of unity, maturity and fullness in our knowledge of Christ. These gifts are always for a wider benefit! But what of their function? What do these people do?[21]

Understanding the fivefold gifts as five kinds of people

Paul writes how these ascension gifts are given to help unite and mature the body of Christ. I think of them as the five strands of Jesus DNA[22]. In the natural our biological DNA has two strands that form a double helix molecule with all our genetic information encoded within it. Jesus 'grace' DNA has five strands. It makes sense that Jesus has placed his own 'grace' DNA within his own body with a specific genetic coding for the purpose of making his body whole, united and mature. For this reason, I consider these fives graces to be of a different nature and importance than the grace gifts and manifestation gifts that we see in Romans and Corinthians.

Jesus is our ultimate role model for all five of these grace-gifts. He is the Great Apostle (Hebr 3.1), the Prophet (Matt 21.11), the bringer of the Good News (Lk 4.18, 43), the Good Shepherd (John 10.11) and the Teacher (John 13.13). In him we see the fulfillment of these five gifts. It is fitting for us to remember that he gives gifts that reflect his own DNA for the purpose of building up his own body. If we want to understand how each gift works then Jesus offers us the best example for us to learn from.

As I read Scripture and the accounts of the early church, it seems to me that the fivefold gifts in Ephesians 4:11 describe the functions of people and not simply titles (or offices) of leadership. I think the distinction is important. I do believe that people who have been appointed within the church to 'offices' of leadership under the guidance of the Holy Spirit will function in one (or more) of these gifts.[23] However, I think it is unhelpful to *only* speak about the 'office' of apostle or prophet etc. as if it were only a position of privilege rather than a function. The reason is that Christ gave these gifts to 'each one of us' and not just to leaders![24]

To speak only of the 'office' of apostle or prophet can imply that Ephesians 4:11 applies only to a special few people and points to a hierarchy that I don't believe exists in Jesus' upside down Kingdom.[25] I actually think that all members in the body exhibit traits of one or more of these functions to some degree or another, just like every organ and cell in your body carry the common DNA of your body, and this is one of the main reasons that I believe the Church needs to recover these Ascension grace-giftings for all of it's members if it is to fully mature.

It is Jesus who gives people their divine assignment and only he gives them the authority they need to accomplish their assignment. The difference will be the place in the body to which they have been assigned and the degree of authority, maturity and anointing they are able to exhibit.

Someone who functions with an apostolic grace and is called to plant a small missional community in a rural setting might have a very different looking influence and anointing compared to someone who is called by God to be an apostolic leader and overseer of an international network of churches and who may be recognized widely as holding the Office of an Apostle. Both are to be honored in the body for the place they have been assigned and both may well be functioning in an apostolic way but they will look very different while still exhibiting common 'apostolic' traits. Each has been given a different sphere of influence and a different measure of anointing. This is critical to comprehend. We will do a great deal of harm in the body of Christ if we continue to present 'big church' and 'influential leaders' as the only model of the Christian life that every Christian should aspire to. We need Christians who understand their measure of grace and the sphere of influence within which they have been called to faithfully exercise it. We need kingdom minded believers in every walk of life at every level of influence bringing the life and righteousness of Christ to all of society so that the nations will be blessed.

It is vital that we learn to look around the body and it's various expressions and ask the question, 'do we see these five grace-gifts expressed in a life giving way that equips the body and builds maturity and unity'. Five fold gifting is not a badge of honor or a sign of privilege. It is people-as-gifts given to serve the body to bring maturity and unity and the fullness of the knowledge of Christ. Remember that the early church has to deal with counterfeits of all these people. Paul argued with false apostles, Jesus warned of false prophets, Jude warned against false shepherds who only fed themselves and Peter warned against false teachers.

Let's now take a look at each of these five fold graces in a little more detail.

Gifts from Jesus - apostles

Apostle word literally means 'sent one' from the greek word *apostolos*, i.e. one who has been sent by the authority of another. Prior to its appearance in the New Testament this infrequently used greek word could apply equally to a seafaring cargo ('sent' goods), the naval ship or fleet that carried it ('sent' transportation), or even the commander of the naval fleet ('sent person'). The key idea was that of being sent.[26]

According to Greek language scholars the word *apostolos* in non-biblical historical documents in some cases "refers to persons who are dispatched for a specific purpose, and the context determines the status or function expressed in such terms as 'ambassador, delegate, messenger'. It is this isolated usage that is preferred in the NT with nuances peculiar to its literature'.[27]"

In the New Testament, the word *apostle* carries a somewhat new meaning and is used much more frequently than in any non biblical material. The word appears over 75 times in the New Testament suggesting that it has a significant place in the mind of the NT authors Paul and Luke (remember that Paul and his traveling companion Dr Luke, between them wrote more than half to the New Testament).

In the gospels, we read that Jesus designated his twelve closest disciples as apostles and sent them out with his authority to proclaim the Kingdom and do the work of the Kingdom in the places where they were sent. This is the basis of how Jesus used the word apostle to describe these particular disciples.

> "And he called to him his twelve disciples and *gave them authority* over unclean spirits, to cast them out, and to heal every disease and every affliction. The names of the twelve *apostles* are these: first, Simon, who is called Peter, and Andrew his brother; James the son of Zebedee, and John his brother; Philip and Bartholomew; Thomas and Matthew the tax collector; James the son of Alphaeus, and Thaddaeus; Simon the Zealot, and Judas Iscariot, who betrayed him.
>
> These twelve *Jesus sent out*, instructing them, "Go nowhere

among the Gentiles and enter no town of the Samaritans, but go rather to the lost sheep of the house of Israel. And <u>proclaim as you go, saying, 'The kingdom of heaven is at hand.</u>' Heal the sick, raise the dead, cleanse lepers, cast out demons. You received without paying; give without pay." (Matthew 10.1-8).

Jesus sends out his twelve Apostles with his delegated authority and a specific mission.

We later discover that there are others in the newly birthed Mediterranean churches that are referred to as apostles as well. It seems that Paul used the same greek word in 1 Corinthians 8.23 when he writes of his fellow workers as *'messengers of the churches'* and again in Philippians 2.25 when referring to his fellow worker Epaphroditus. Paul can unashamedly refer to himself as an Apostle of Christ (big 'A') as he encountered the Risen Christ and was given a specific mission by Jesus while referring to others in the churches as apostles/messengers (little 'a') by using the same word. They include people like Barnabas (Acts 14.14), Titus (2 Cor 8.23) and James the brother of Jesus (Gal 1.19), demonstrating that while Jesus did indeed uniquely appoint his twelve disciples as Apostles, there is a wider role of apostle which was not limited to those twelve men. Indeed, we also read of a woman apostle called Junia in Romans 16.7.[28]

It appears that the broader group of New Testament apostles were involved in establishing and helping grow new communities of Jesus followers around the Mediterranean and teaching them according to the 'Apostolic witness', by that I mean the first hand account of Jesus teaching handed down from the first disciples, the twelve *Apostles*.

Many apostles seem to travel geographically and are associated to church planting teams. Several apostles, including Paul, were involved in running their own business in the marketplace as a source of funding themselves. The common thread seems to be that they were all involved in the proclamation of the Kingdom and the establishing of the nascent Christian communities.

I think this background can inform the most basic understanding of what it means to be *apostolic* today:- to know you are sent with a mission by the authority of the one who sends you (the Holy Spirit) and that you proclaim and demonstrate the good news of the Kingdom in the place where the King sends you.

This often requires 'apostles' to be resourceful starters and builders who have a God given vision to start something that didn't exist previously. They often pioneer new ministries. They break new ground and push beyond comfortable boundaries. That is why we often hear the word 'entrepreneurial' used when describing apostolic people and ministries. I can also understand why in certain parts of the church modern day missionaries[29] have been considered as the 'replacement' for apostles going into new cultures to break the ground for establishing a Kingdom stronghold.

I believe that as apostles are recognized, released and honored in the body then we will see an accelerated increase in Kingdom advancement. When I see people who function *effectively* as apostles today, I notice that they are not interested in proclaiming their own importance or having the title "Apostle". I do think that apostles can have different levels of anointing and maturity. As a result I think we do see people in significant leadership offices who are apostles, but in my humble opinion, an apostle better describes how they function rather than specifically denoting a church office or 'title'.[30]

Since apostles have a strong sense of purpose, it is usually in their nature to send others out too. Hence church planting and missions equipping is often considered to be apostolic work. Apostles are usually 'big picture' people who present a vision of what the Kingdom of God is like. Being around an apostle can be exhilarating, inspiring and exhausting all at the same time! That's why the other four grace-gifts (prophets, evangelists, shepherds and teachers) bring a very necessary balance to apostolic ministry that complements it. Isn't it interesting that Jesus chose to give a complementary community of gifts in order to build up the body!

The transformation we are seeing in this current season globally as apostolic leaders are being recognized and honored is simply a restoration of something that has been missing for too long in the body of Christ. Apostolic leadership is not about earthly power or hierarchy. Jesus challenged his disciples about their worldly views on power and told them that to be great in the Kingdom is to be the servant of all. Rather apostolic leadership is about alignment. It is about pursuing some aspect of 'on earth as it is in heaven' that brings about tangible change. The early church called their apostles 'Church Fathers'. Apostolic leaders should be spiritual father and mother figures to the church, raising up the next generation to take new ground. The apostle Paul's letters are a testimony to the number of people he raised up and released into ministry. while we have canonized Paul's letters, (without doubt his ministry more than any other transformed the early church around the Mediterranean), Paul never considers that the church exists to support his ministry, rather time and again he reminds the churches to whom he writes of how he has worked and suffered on their behalf to help them mature and grow.

Unfortunately, I am sure that there are examples of abuses of power and privilege in the body of Christ that would cause many to throw the baby out with the bathwater. However, the response to error must not be more error! Selfishness, pride and greed are not exclusive to those promoting fivefold ministry! They are traits found throughout all of fallen humanity and all expressions of church. Alan Hirsch helpfully points out that even the New Testament refers to 'false apostles', i.e. people whose claim to apostleship did not seem credible even early on in the life of the church. The Apostle Paul's response was not to reject apostleship, but rather to point to the authoritative validity of his own apostolic ministry demonstrated by his humble, arduous service and his legacy in the churches he established and nurtured.[31]

In their book *The Shaping Of Things To Come*, missiologists Michael Frost and Alan Hirsch offer the following definition – "the apostolic function [is] usually conducted trans-locally, pioneers new missional works and oversees their development".[32] Frost and Hirsch are strong advocates for the missional nature of the work which apostles are called to. This is especially important in the increasingly post-Christendom cultural landscape in which we find ourselves today.

I also appreciate Michael Brodeur's analogy of an apostle as 'Builder'. Commenting on 1 Corinthians 3.10-11, Michael writes that the Apostle Paul is basically saying of his own apostolic ministry "I'm the general contractor who's seen the blueprint and who's hiring the subcontractors to get the work done. Everyone needs to come into this process in a way that honors the blueprint I'm seeing".[33]

So apostles know they are sent, they know the authority of the one who sends them and they know the mission on which they have been sent. They call the body to enter into God's mission[34]. They are pioneers, builders, culture makers and visionaries. They think in terms of opportunities to advance. They create momentum and vision that prevents the church from becoming a lifeless monument.

Gifts from Jesus - prophets

Prophets[35] are people who speak on God's behalf. They are the covenant stewards. They keep calling us back to covenant relationship with God.

Throughout the history of God's people, prophets have been a major way through which God has spoken to his people. Much maligned and often misunderstood, the function of the prophet is to call God's people back to faithfulness to his covenant. This can happen in many different ways, but most simply it involves bringing a revelation of the truth about God and what He has said in order to re-align people who have wandered from that plumb-line. Even the New Testament guidelines for prophetic ministry (that it should encourage, exhort and edify) are essentially placing the revelation about who God is and what he says about a situation in front of people so that they can respond by affirming this truth and rejecting any lies they have believed. It is a call to covenant faithfulness; an invitation to hear God's voice to us and a challenge to obey what we hear.

Now prophets can minister through speech, art, music, song, dreams or prophetic actions. Many of the Old Testament prophets seem to have spoken in poetic and very creative ways. They will often speak out against injustice calling us back to a biblical standard for Kingdom justice. They might be any age, with or without an education, in positions of church leadership or perhaps part of the body at large. Some prophets love being alone with God (so it is not unusual to come across prophets who are a little socially awkward around people!). Sometimes prophets may bring revelation of things that have not yet happened, but they are equally likely to reveal God's perspective on what has happened or is happening. To think of a socially awkward individual who looks heavenward and dramatically declares 'thus saith the Lord' is to have a very limited understanding on how prophets function.

Some church movements see prophets as primarily voices against injustice. Other church movements see prophets more like future seeing visionaries. These are the two ends of the spectrum. They both bring value and maturity to the body, but one with out the other brings a very anaemic perspective to the grace gift of prophets.

However, prophets should ultimately be bringers of hope, carrying the heart of Jesus to his people. Even if they are calling sinful people back to God through repentance, the hopefulness of their message will be the steadfast love and mercy of God. There really is no place for the 'prophets of doom and gloom' amongst God's people.

Apostles and prophets both tend to be heaven focused. Prophets need to be connected to and aligned with apostolic vision so they don't simply become unattached critics. Prophets may well love spending time by themselves in God's presence, so they may need to be pastored to grow in healthy relationships. Prophets can see God's perspective on a situation or person and call it out bringing hope and encouragement.

I have heard stories from people growing up in very religious pentecostal churches who feared prophets visiting their church because they would expose peoples sin. For sure, holiness is part of what it means to be in covenant with God, but shaming people is not the modus operandi of Jesus. Conviction (the work of Holy Spirit) is very different from condemnation. There is no condemnation for those who are in Christ Jesus.

I sat in a church leadership gathering recently where a prophet gave out very specific and detailed words of knowledge, prophecies and words of encouragement to around ten individuals in a room of nearly a thousand leaders. What was exciting was that while 990 of us did not receive a prophetic word we were <u>all</u> massively encouraged by this man's ministry. His words brought hope, increased our faith levels and re-focused us all on Jesus mercy and sovereignty. Now this man has a significant leadership role within the body of Christ and is able to minister in many nations. But I have friends who function as prophets in their own local congregations, in their businesses or even in their own small groups. Their anointing and measure of influence all look very different. All are gifts from Christ to the church and they all seek to build up the body and equip them for ministry, as each of them prophecy in accordance with the measure of faith they have.

There are so many good resources available today on the subject of prophetic ministry. As God has been restoring his prophetic DNA to the church at large there have been many mistakes and errors to learn from. But remember, all mistakes are a learning opportunity. As I said earlier, to react to an error with another error doesn't move anyone closer to the truth!

All the five functions are given to bring unity and maturity to the body, equipping the saints for them to do the work of ministry. The prophet will often do this by being an agitator or out-of-the-box thinker who challenges the status quo when the status quo falls short of covenant faithfulness.

Gifts from Jesus - evangelists

The word evangelist comes from a Greek word *euaggelizō* that literally means to bring good news or glad tidings. Jesus himself came proclaiming the good news that the Kingdom of God was at hand (Mark 1.14-15). An evangelist is a bringer of good news.

Along with the apostles and prophets, evangelists bring movement and transformation to the community of God by keeping it focused outside of itself. Evangelists have a passion to engage with people who don't know God. They want as many people as possible to hear their message because they believe whole-heartedly that it is a message worth hearing. They are, as Michael Brodeur calls them, the 'recruiters' for the Kingdom.

Now let's apply what we have been saying about the measure of grace Jesus gives. Some might be apportioned grace to function as evangelists to huge crowds filling stadiums. I think of the late Reinhard Bonnke who preached to millions in Africa during his gospel crusades, or the late Dr Billy Graham who has preached to the multitudes around the world for over half a century. I also think of street evangelists who often declare the gospel boldly to passers-by. I think of a retired lady in my church who is happy to share the good news of what Jesus has done for her with her friends at her local ladies fitness center, with her neighbors and even at her fifty year high school reunion. Each one of these dear saints is functioning as an evangelist proclaiming good news, but each operates faithfully with a different measure of grace that they received.

The body of Christ desperately needs evangelists to equip the saints in how to invite and challenge unbelievers to respond to God's call to follow Christ, as well as to remind the church just how good the good news of Jesus Kingdom is! Many of us have forgotten.

We also need to see that evangelists are not simply type 'A' extrovert personalities (though I have met many who are). The danger is that this can be the only model of evangelism that is modeled to the body, i.e. going up to complete strangers and striking up conversations with them about matters of spirituality and eternity, in the manner of a traveling salesperson 'selling' eternal life. Instead, we need evangelists who can equip and activate all the saints (including us introverts!) in sharing the good news with the people of peace that we regularly engage with as we go about our lives, with words of comfort or challenge, even speaking prophetically, as well as acts of kindness all of which can powerfully reveal the goodness of God to those around us softening their hearts to the convicting work of Holy Spirit.

An evangelist burns with a passion to see Romans 10.13-15 in action.

> For *"everyone who calls on the name of the Lord will be saved."*
> *How then will they call on him in whom they have not believed?*
> *And how are they to believe in him of whom they have never*
> *heard? And how are they to hear without someone preaching?*
> *And how are they to preach unless they are sent? As it is written,*
> *"How beautiful are the feet of those who preach the good news!"*

Part of the job of an evangelist should be to help the church to answer the question, 'what does the Good News of the Gospel of the Kingdom look like to the people I am sharing it with'. In other words, while the Gospel does not change, it does need to be contextualized for its listeners. while the centrality of our sin and our need for a Savior is not in question, that is not the fullness of the gospel message that we bring. Jesus brought the good news of the Kingdom of God before he died on a cross but clearly the event of the cross has become central to this good news! We are inviting people into the abundant life that belonging to Jesus' Kingdom brings now and the certainty of the kind of future his Kingdom will bring.

Paul knew how to contextualize his gospel presentations. One day while in Athens, he was invited to come and share his 'strange new' message to a group of Epicurean and Stoic philosophers in the Areopagus. They loved to hear new ideas and Paul's message was certainly new for their ears. Rather than share the message in the same way that he had done with the Jews (which Paul was careful to do in every town he visited), he starts by observing the philosophers practice of having altars to unknown gods and he makes a connection between what they are searching for and what he has to say about the God of creation. He even quotes Greek poetry to them as a means of connecting them to his good news message. The fruit of this was that while some mocked him, a few listened, believed and joined him.[36]

The Gospel is a topsy turvy message for our culture. The way up is the way down! We must lose our lives to find them! The first shall be last and the last shall be first. It will certainly offend many, but we must make sure that we don't become the stumbling block. That includes the way in which we share this wonderful message.

Not everyone contemplates where they will spend eternity. Some people are just trying to live through the trials of today. Others face the daily realities of poverty or injustice. Even the wealthy (who appear to have it all together on the outside) can be crushed internally under the weight of their loneliness and spiritual poverty. While the Gospel is unchangeable, each of these people will connect to a different aspect of the richness of the Gospel as Good News to them. Effective evangelists can bring the message in a way that people can respond to it positively.

Evangelists are necessary to remind the body of Christ that the mission field for the church lies outside of the church. As with each Ascension gift, without the evangelist grace gift, the body cannot come into the fullness of the knowledge of Christ or know true maturity.

Gifts from Jesus - shepherds

The greek word used here is always translated 'shepherd' in scripture, so I have chosen to remain true to that translation. I have deliberately refrained from using the English word 'pastor' (which derives from the Latin word for shepherd) for reasons I will explain shortly.

The shepherd in scripture is a picture of one who cares for, directs and defends a flock. A shepherd has authority through being a servant to those under their care. Jesus describes himself as the 'good Shepherd' in John 10.11. He even lays down his life for his sheep. Ultimately, Jesus is the Great Shepherd of the sheep[37] and those who care for his flock in the church are called to be an example.

If evangelists are comfortable spending lots of time around the lost, then shepherds are comfortable spending their time with people who need nurturing and comforting. They seek to help them grow healthy, to eat well, leading them on safe paths and building healthy relationships. They are moved by compassion to care for people. They help nurture sick and weak sheep back to strength (physically and spiritually).

They are concerned with spiritual formation, helping those in their care demonstrate a fully orbed and developed spirituality. They will be champions of love and hope in the midst of the reality of pain and weakness. Shepherds are no strangers to the messes that their flocks can produce and can incarnate God's presence by simply being with people in their pain. I refer to this as the ministry of 'presence'. It requires laying aside the desire to fix people because of our own discomfort with their pain and being present with people as they confront their pain, in order that they might pass through it to embrace the resurrection life of Christ. Too often we rush to fix people in attempt for them to avoid experiencing pain, but Christ himself did not shy away from pain or sorrow at the Cross. Rather it was the path to resurrection life. The shepherd does not leave people in their mess nor criticize them for experiencing it but exhorts them to follow the Great Shepherd out of their mess into greener pastures.

Psalm 23 is a beautiful picture of the kind of shepherd that the Lord is. It is a wonderful vision for pastoral ministry. I want to highlight one verse that is often overlooked. In verse 2 we read that 'he makes me lie down in green pastures'. Sheep can sometimes get themselves into distress. This can be particularly dangerous for a pregnant ewe. In her distress, she actually puts herself and her unborn lamb at risk. A loving shepherd may actually break the leg of a ewe in distress in order to make them lie down so he can then carry them on his shoulders to safety. It can be a kind of enforced rest. Sometimes, I think God shepherds us in this manner, forcing us to a place of rest so that we can finally desist from our futile ways and receive his comfort and sustenance.

Shepherds are not afraid of conflict, in fact they understand the necessity of healthy conflict for the benefit of the flock. They are not cruel to their flock, but they have sufficient concern for their well being that they will not shy away from removing a sheep out of a potentially dangerous or harmful situation. Comforting includes disciplining. When we take a truly biblical approach to dealing with conflict based on love, honesty, forgiveness, courage and honor we will create healthy environments and healthy relationships.

Shepherds are great at building community and look to bring healing through healthy community. We all know people in the church who look out for people, invite them out for coffee or go and visit the sick and grieving. These are the shepherds. They are by no means always the church leaders!

One of the reasons I am refraining from using the word 'pastor' is because it has become a catch-all term to describe a church leader, but honestly, many church leaders are not shepherds. They may learn to carry out some of the duties of a shepherd (as encouraged in 1 Peter 5:1-5) but often their leadership duties do not give them the time to sit with hurting people and practice the ministry of presence.

We should be careful not to expect every leader to be a shepherd, while at the same time praying that we recognize who amongst the body are called to shepherd the flock.

Shepherds bring the necessary skills of caring for people that apostolic visionaries, who focus on vision and outcomes, often lack. Apostles and evangelists will look upwards and outwards to ensure that shepherds do not become static and inward looking. Shepherds will care for the community to ensure it survives.

Gifts from Jesus - teachers

Along with the shepherds, the teachers bring stability and continuity to the community of God. The role of the teacher is to bring wisdom, understanding and maturity in God's ways to the people of

God. Primarily this is through bringing an understanding of what the Spirit is saying through the Scriptures. A teacher will not just interpret Scripture, but will also incarnate the truth of Scripture. In other words, a teacher's authority is based on what he/she models not just on their intellectual knowledge bank. This is in keeping with Jesus role as a disciple making Rabbi.

Jesus is the role model for this grace gift and refers to himself as 'the Teacher' in Matt 26.18. Jesus was noted as one who taught with unusual authority. He did not just convey clever intellectual ideas; he demonstrated what he had just preached by casting out demons and healing the sick. He taught using story telling techniques and visual demonstrations (compare this to our modern western teaching practices in our churches).

The role of the teacher in ancient eastern culture is very different from our western concept of a teacher. In the west we have settled for the transfer of knowledge and information as a substitute for being 'trained' by a master teacher.

Effective teachers help you to understand and put into practice God's ways. What was complicated and unclear becomes clear and understandable in the hands of a good teacher.

In the church, good teachers will open up the scriptures in such a way that it makes us hungry to open them for ourselves. They are infectious in their enthusiasm for what they are teaching. They also have an ability to help us inhabit the story of Scripture. JR Woodward says 'the teacher finds creative ways to immerse the community in Scripture so they can faithfully live in God's story'.[38] Teachers help us to orient ourselves in God's truths.

It has been common for the shepherding and teaching gift to be found together. In the nuance of the greek language these two functions actually share one definite article, i.e. shepherd-teacher almost appears to be one function. However, we see these gifts distinguished elsewhere, so I am cautious about concluding that they must always appear together. A friend of mine helped me see the relationship between these two functions when she said that the shepherd may be concerned about love more than truth, while teachers may focus on truth more than love. In this sense, the two need to go hand in hand whether that is in one person or more typically in unity amongst the fivefold community.

This value for truth means that teachers seek to provide an anchor in the Scriptures for the beliefs and practices of the church body - the fancy words for this are orthodoxy (right belief) and orthopraxy (right practice). They will speak out against teaching that deviates from or obscures the truths of Scripture. Remember, that the early church had to resist false teachers (2 Peter 2.1).

Within the fivefold callings teachers need to complement the visionary roles of the apostles and prophets to bring solid, biblical understanding to apostolic vision and prophetic revelation, which in turn keeps the teacher relevant to what the Spirit is doing and saying.

Wrapping up the gifts from Jesus

I have alluded already to the fact that the apostles, prophets and evangelists tend to be the agitators who provide momentum to the body, while the shepherds and teachers operate more like builders who bring stability to the community. Mike Breen uses the idea of 'pioneers' to describe apostles, prophets, evangelists and 'settlers' to describe shepherds and teachers. Pioneers push forward into new unexplored territory expanding boundaries and vistas, but unless settlers come behind and build out protection and stability, the ground gained by the pioneers will soon be lost again. Both are necessary. It is important to see how necessary all five gifts are for the church to come into the fulness of it's maturity and purpose, something that I cannot overstate.

This leads me to wonder whether one person is 'stuck' with having just one of these functions or can they have more than one? Once again I have found Mike Breen to be helpful in understanding how to respond to this question. Just as I have already stated that one person can function in more than one of these roles, Mike develops this a little further. He says that most of us usually have a strong primary function (or calling). This is our most clearly demonstrated five fold function and will often drive our vocational decisions. It is the function that makes us feel most alive; it is the one we do without thinking about. Mike calls this our 'Base' Ministry. It's what we keep returning to.

However, depending on the seasons of life and ministry roles that we may find ourselves in, we need to learn how to operate from a different function. This secondary function is called our 'Phase' ministry. In other words it grows depending on the phase of life and ministry situation that we are in. Our phase ministry is somewhat situational in nature, but that does not make it any less permanent. The lessons we learn in how to operate in our phase ministries mature us, sharpen our base ministry and contribute to making us more competent in our broader ministry.

Leaders, in particular, need to understand this ebb and flow of operating in base and phase ministries so that they can become well rounded. while I would always champion team leadership, which fosters the kind of interdependence that is depicted in Ephesians 4.11, I think the best leaders understand and have some experience and awareness in each of the different functions. This process develops high capacity leaders who are able to recognize and work with other five-fold leaders effectively.

As an example, I led worship for many years at the church I attended in my twenties and thirties. During this time, I would say that this developed my phase ministry of 'prophet'. I learned how to be sensitive to the Holy Spirit and to present what I was hearing to the congregation in a way that was life giving and encouraging.

In a later season, I took on an eldership role within the church. This forced me to press into a more shepherding phase that I had not operated in before, as well as beginning to explore my teaching function.

In my current role as a full time pastor on a church staff, I am primarily functioning as teacher and shepherd. Can I still function prophetically? Yes, absolutely I can and I frequently do, but that is not my current phase ministry. My base ministry is actually teacher. It was sort of dormant for many years, in a way I had not realized. I am wired to try and understand things so I can convey complex ideas in a simple way to others. I did that for years as a structural engineer; I did it when I led worship; I am a lifelong learner and want to understand things so I can help explain them to other people in a way that they can understand too.

So does this mean that I can 'choose' my fivefold gifting? I don't think so. The different contexts I have found myself in have all been part of how God has led me. They have been part of God's purpose for shaping me. I didn't simply wake up one morning and think "hey,

I'd like to be an elder in the church so I can develop my shepherd-teacher phase ministry". I responded to the leading of the Holy Spirit, discerned prayerfully in community and then operated within the *measure* of grace I had been given. If I had moved in presumption I would quickly have found myself ill equipped to do what I hadn't been called to do! Remember, Paul roots his short teaching on the five-fold ministry in the context of being members of Christ's body. As soon as we detach ourselves from the context of community and the body, we have stepped out of the realm in which the fivefold ministry was designed for.

A few years back, our church leadership team used a couple of survey tools to help us to clearly identify where our primary and secondary callings lay, and how that impacted the roles we are fulfilling, as well as helping us to see our differences as a gift that can help mature us. It was insightful not only to clarify how each person functioned but for several people it was also very helpful in better understanding themselves bringing awareness as to why they thrive/struggle in different settings.

Most people discover that they have a strong primary gifting followed closely by a secondary gifting that helps shapes the expression of their primary gift. To this degree, we might learn in due course to understand the subtle nuances of being a shepherd-teacher, compared to a shepherd-apostle, or an apostle-prophet compared to an apostle-evangelist.[39]

Aligning the saints

"And he gave the apostles, the prophets, the evangelists, the shep-

> herds and teachers, <u>to equip</u> the saints for the work of ministry,
> for building up the body of Christ..."

An interesting word appears in Ephesians 4.12. The NIV and ESV translates it as 'to equip'. It speaks to the purpose of the fivefold functions. They are given to equip the saints (i.e. the people of God) so that they are able to do the work of service and ministry. Did you get that? The point of the fivefold is to launch other people into ministry, which is the good works that God has prepared in advance for every believer (Eph 2.10). God didn't give the five-fold gifts to the body so that the saints could serve the ministry of the few.

Remember, Jesus modeled servant leadership to his disciples. What God has given to us is for us to pass on to other people. It is in giving away what we have received that we are blessed. That's why Jesus taught that it is more blessed to give than to receive.

So what does it look like to equip the saints for ministry? Paul certainly trained those around him by discipling them and giving them a living example to imitate. There was doubtless life-on-life discipleship going on all the time with Paul as he travelled with teams and stayed in the homes of the people of peace he met. But what did this equipping look like to Paul? The Greek word used here *(katartismos)* has an interesting meaning. It can be translates as maturing, aligning, healing, restoring and perfecting (the KJV translation). It was used as a medical term describing the setting, re-aligning and healing of a broken bone. In other words, re-aligning something that is out of alignment in order that it might be healed and made whole again. Paul is saying that the apostles, prophets etc are sent to bring a re-alignment to something that is out of alignment. They bring a healing and maturing to the body. Who are they re-aligning and to what are they re-aligning them? They are aligning the saints (the members of the body) to the head of the body (Jesus) for God's mission. In other words, perfecting the saints for the work of ministry. Whose ministry? God's ministry... through us all!

Now before some of you switch off and decide that you don't feel called to work for the church, nowhere does Paul imply that this ministry is to be found only in the church?

Nowhere.

Jesus ministered wherever he found himself. Yes, at times that was in the synagogue, but at other times it was hanging out at the village well, or at a dinner party thrown in his honor. Similarly Paul, who frequently went first to the synagogue to minister found himself debating in the market place and with the city officials. If you presume that God is only calling you to serve in the church then you have just written off the possibility of God using you for about 165 hours of your 168 hour week (assuming that you attend one service on a Sunday and one mid week small group meeting). No wonder so much of the church is ineffective in mission. We only try to recruit people into church ministry. Fivefold ministry aligns people with God's ministry and helps them to discover what Kingdom works God has prepared for them.

I believe this alignment is threefold. We are to be aligned with Christ who is the head of the body; we are to be aligned to the apostolic vision provided through the apostolic function; finally, we are to be aligned correctly within the body of Christ to one another. So let's explore what these three alignments look like.

Aligning to Christ the head

Quite simply this means to be under the headship of Christ. To be a disciple of Jesus is to be submitted to him in recognition of his status as the Son of God, as head of his body (the Church) and as the one seated at the right hand of the Father. The Father has given all authority to Jesus. Jesus authorizes his followers to share in his mission. That requires us to be submitted to his authority first (SUB-mission to Christ leads to the great CO-mission).

A Roman centurion encountered Jesus in Capernaum. This military man understood authority and recognized the authority Jesus had. He chose to honor and submit to Jesus' authority by simply accepting that if Jesus said that his servant would be healed, then that was good enough for him to act on. Jesus was so impressed with this response that he noted that he had never seen such faith from anyone in Israel (Matthew 8.5-13).

The fivefold gifts, which are themselves a representation of the character of Christ, are given out by a victorious Jesus leading a host of captives, equipping and aligning God's people to his victorious headship; so firstly we must align ourselves to King Jesus.

Aligning to apostolic vision

We have already examined how the role of the apostolic is to bring the blueprint of heaven's vision. The apostolic vision is therefore 'on earth as it is in heaven'. But in each setting God needs the apostolic function to articulate what that looks like. To be effectively implemented the apostolic vision is going to need the prophets, evangelists, shepherds and teachers as well. This is a family affair!

The fivefold ministry therefore brings the saints into alignment with the apostolic vision, equipping them to find their place and role in the Kingdom's strategic blueprint. It is in this area that much of the church suffers from a lack of connection to apostolic leaders who bring that vision. When the church is primarily led by shepherds and teachers then Kingdom vision is often limited to simply caring for a flock. Hear my heart on this: shepherds and teachers are absolutely necessary, valuable and non-negotiable parts of the fivefold ministry. But two-fold ministry is not what Jesus had in mind for his body! Not every local church is led by an apostolic leader, and nor does it need to be. However, shepherd-teacher leaders need to be aligned to an apostolic vision. There has been an absence of healthy apostolic leadership in some denominations and streams and I think this explains why more relational based apostolic networks have been exploding in many parts of the church around the world. Of course, we have to navigate the dangers of unhealthy, self-proclaimed apostles, but so did Paul (just read 2 Corinthians, where Paul has to combat the threat of self-proclaimed 'super-apostles'). It's nothing new and it is certainly not an excuse for ignoring the importance of apostolic alignment. I've had the privilege of working with an apostolic leader, Dr Che Ahn, for much of the past decade. In his words,

> "To be apostolicly aligned we must carry the heart of our leader or apostle… this is not submission to some heavy handed authority. It does not mean we are to walk in uniformity with leadership, or always be in complete agreement… there is room and indeed need for diversity in our alignment and unity. In fact, times of disagreement are when our alignment is most deeply tested. We do not commit ourselves to blind obedience, but to honoring our mutual values and mission above our temporary conflicts[40]."

An important question to ask yourself (as an individual and a church community) is 'what is the apostolic vision that I am aligned with?' This is one of the ways that we are to be connected to the apostles in the body.

Aligned within the body

This fourth alignment simply means understanding our role and position in the body. By 'position' I am not thinking through the lens of hierarchy or status, but rather I'm thinking about which part in the body am I? Where am I called to function? If I am a kidney, I am of little use if I position myself within the leg of the body. If an eye, then I am no use settled amongst the internal organs! My analogy is a little crude, but I think you get my point. In fact, Paul uses exactly this metaphor a few verses later in chapter four.

> *"We are to grow up in every way into him who is the head, into Christ, from whom the whole body, joined and held together by every joint with which it is equipped [lit. 'fit together'], when each part is working properly, makes the body grow so that it builds itself up in love". (Eph 4.15-16).*

It is vital that we understand that we exist as part of a community. In fact, the imagery is clear. We are no use apart from the body nor are we likely to survive apart from the body. We are made for community, we are made for connection with others, and we are made to work for the good of others. This kingdom culture is counter-cultural to our very individualistic and self-centered western culture. Part of the way that we align ourselves within the body is to honor all the different parts, just as Paul describes to the Corinthians (1 Cor 12.21-27), and to recognize the ways in which they contribute to the body overall. "For no one ever hated his own flesh, but nourishes and cherishes it, just as Christ does the church, because we are members of his body" Ephesians 5.29-30.

Helping the body to mature

> "... to equip the saints for the work of ministry, that is, to build
> up the body of Christ, until we all attain to the unity of the faith
> and of the knowledge of the Son of God —a **mature** person, attain-
> ing to the measure of Christ's full stature." (Ephesians 4:12–13
> NET)

One of the goals of the ascension gifts is to bring the body of Christ
into maturity.

For a long time, much of the church has relegated apostles and
prophets to the history of the pages of scripture, while pastors and
teacher have been accepted roles in throughout the history of the
church. Itinerant evangelists seemed to be tolerated as long as they
directed the souls they won towards the pastors and teachers in the
churches.

Many western churches have embraced this twofold model of
church leadership in the shepherd-teacher ministry. As we have seen
in the previous chapter, while these functions are vitally important for
the health of the church, they cannot fulfill all of the functions of the
five fold gifts. If the ultimate goal is maturity and unity, this will not
be accomplished by only utilizing two of the five Ascension gifts in
the body. All five are needed to accomplish this task. Meanwhile, the
rise of the self-titled Apostolic-Prophetic movement, which is to be
applauded for bringing attention back to two overlooked and undervalued gifts, flies dangerously close to simply swapping which two-
fold ministry it is promoting. Nothing less than five-fold ministry will

bring the church to the maturity that Christ is waiting for.

In the last century, following the rise of the Pentecostal, Charismatic and Third Wave movements there has been a renewed interest in trying to understand the roles of apostles, prophets, evangelists, shepherds and teachers in the church today.[41] It seems that in the eighteenth and nineteenth centuries the Church witnessed a sort of restoration of the gift of the evangelist as great preaching revivals broke out and then subsequently as missions movements were established, while in much of the twentieth century God was beginning the process of restoring prophets to the church and then subsequently the apostolic ministry. There remains much debate and even controversy over the validity of modern day apostles and prophets. For the record, I believe that all five functions are gifts to the church for today and are given for the purpose of building up the body into maturity. It is precisely because I believe that the church has not yet attained the 'measure of the stature of the fullness of Christ' that I believe these five gifts are absolutely necessary in the church today.

What is now happening is that we are beginning to see how all five of these functions knit together to create a healthy and life giving expression of the body of Christ. There are some church communities that are modeling this re-engagement with the five fold ministry very well, but I can't help feel that we have yet to see a full and mature expression of the fivefold ministry in the church at large. It is my prayer that we will not have to wait too long.

I want to offer a few thoughts on how we might navigate the process of helping people to mature into the fullness of their Jesus DNA. Maturity in this sense does not relate to age but more the sense of fulfilling your purpose.

The apostle Paul speaks repeatedly of honoring people in his letters, even calling the church in Rome to 'outdo one another in showing honor' (Romans 12.10). A pastor I respect once said that in a culture of honor we *celebrate who a person is without stumbling over who they are not'*. In other words, we shouldn't criticize someone who has not yet learned to be mature; rather we should learn how to help them to be mature! Can you imagine a parent who constantly criticizes their child for not being an adult? That would be ludicrous, if not abusive! A loving parent will train their child in the way they should go so that they become mature. Discipline is born out of love and seeks to bring wholeness and maturity. So why would we think it works any differently in the church? When we come across someone who is immature in their calling we should not criticize them. Instead, from a place of love we bring grace and truth to them, training them and bringing them to a place of maturity. In other words, we see the potential and celebrate it, rather than stumbling over their immaturity.

If Christ has given grace to each one of us, then we will need to learn to increasingly inhabit that grace as we grow more into the likeness of Christ. That means we will need to learn to mature in our calling and gifting.

What follows are some thoughts on what immaturity and blindspots we might experience and possible ways to grow into maturity.[42] These ideas are offered as potential areas to explore with individuals and teams. They are by no means exhaustive nor will they apply to every person in every situation.. Remember, regardless of our grace gift, we are each called to be faithful disciples of Jesus following in his cruciform shaped victorious life. If these gifts have been given at large to the body, then we must understand how to disciple these people-as-gifts into their own maturity so that in turn they can help bring the body into maturity.

Helping apostles mature

Earlier in this chapter I mentioned some frequently observed traits in those graced as apostles. They are commonly visionaries with a big picture mindset. They can be highly motivated people with a very strong sense of purpose (they have been sent, remember). Because they usually have a clear mission in mind they usually value the change and transformation that needs to take place in order to see their mission accomplished. It is not uncommon for apostles to love building organizations that serve the goal of accomplishing their big picture vision.

But what could be potential blindspots in immature apostles? Well for some, they may have a tendency to use people simply as a means of achieving their goals. This is why apostles need to learn from shepherds the value of caring for people and what is in their hearts, and not just using them for what is in their hands.

Big picture people are often not afraid of failure. Failure is just a step along the path to success. But the inability to discern 'good' ideas from 'God' ideas can lead to squandering the resources of a community who do not all see things the same way.

Purpose driven people can be prone to being impatient with others, either because they operate at a much more energetic pace, or because they fear not being in control of the process that will help them achieve their goals.

It can be helpful therefore for growing apostles to engage in relevant spiritual disciplines that will help them mature. These might include learning to value people for what is in their hearts and not just for how they can be of 'use'. They will also mature by learning to practice discern the difference between good ideas and inspired ideas within the context of community. This will often require learning the discipline of listening to others with differing viewpoints along with practicing patience. Finally, developing apostles will benefit from learning to empower other people as they work towards their goals so as to avoid the pitfall of control.

Helping prophets mature

What are some of the frequently observed qualities in those graced as prophets? It is not unusual for prophets to be highly creative folks, who embrace the mysticism and symbolism of heaven. This may be expressed through creative arts, or even just their out of the box thinking.

Some prophets might be very justice oriented, concerned and outspoken for the justice of God's Kingdom to be released in situations where injustice and oppression is obvious. Other prophets might be particularly future oriented, constantly thinking about where things will be further down the road.

But what could be potential blindspots in immature prophets? For those who are not yet mature in their embrace of mysticism there can be a tendency towards dualism, in other word, valuing 'spiritual' things over 'earthly' things. Some immature prophets can fall into the Corinthian trap of becoming elitist [because 'I heard from God'], when in reality the contribution of others is equally honorable before the

Lord. This pride can manifest in valuing intuition above validation i.e. a prophet doesn't submit their words to testing by others. Finally, some immature prophet may fear organization or structure that brings accountability because of an over emphasis on spontaneity.

It can be helpful therefore for growing prophets to engage in relevant spiritual disciplines that will help them mature. Helpful spiritual disciplines might look like developing spiritual accountability through prophetic mentoring communities. In addition, all prophets should be committed to faithful engagement with Scriptures in order that the necessary plumb line of discernment is in place. And finally, growing prophets need to develop humility especially towards the leaders in their church communities. Prophets may well receive insight and revelation from God, but they may not be the ones that God has tasked with being responsible for leading and caring for the wider community. In this case, humility looks like honoring those who are gifted and called differently.

Helping evangelists mature

What are some of the frequently observed attributes in those graced as evangelists? Evangelists are commonly great connectors and communicators who are skilled in recruiting and motivating people. A mature evangelist is comfortable connecting with complete strangers because of their passion for both people and the gospel.

But what could be potential blindspots in immature evangelists? Well, immaturity in someone who is accomplished at being persuasive could lead to manipulation and self-promotion. Remember a mature evangelist has a heart for the lost, but a zealous evangelist who has not yet captured the Father's heart for the lost can be motivated out of self promotion rather than service.

Sometimes the unreasonable expectations placed on evangelists to 'bring in the lost' can mean they substitute 'winning souls' over 'making disciples'. Any sense of unresolved insecurity can compromise the integrity of their gospel proclamation in order to 'get results'. Finally, an immature evangelist can be so fired up on zeal that they live permanently in a state of anxious urgency which exhausts them both physically and mentally leading to potential spiritual compromise or burnout.

Therefore some helpful spiritual disciplines for developing evangelists include trusting Holy Spirit to do the work of conviction and salvation as well as having a high value for being discipled and making disciples (especially empowering others in evangelism). Furthermore, learning to rest and wait patiently on the Lord will allow evangelists to flow from a place of non-anxious presence. This can be particularly helpful in learning to discern where Holy Spirit is already at work and therefore where there is a spiritual harvest ready for gathering.

Helping shepherds mature

What are some of the common traits we see in mature shepherds? Most people would recognize that a good shepherd is a people lover, sensitive to the needs of others and able to be a non-anxious presence when others are in distress. Mature shepherds notice people who are on the fringes and can reach out 'for the one' and still have a concern for the whole flock. The overflow of their love and calmness creates healthy and stable relationships among the community.

But shepherds who have not yet matured can also have blindspots.

A common problem is that they can succumb to people pleasing and therefore compromise their commitment to prioritizing God, for example when moments of confrontation need to happen, they may avoid it for fear of 'offending people'. Immature shepherds can fall into the trap of needing to 'fix' people to feel good about themselves, turning people in to projects. This usually goes hand in hand with having poor relational boundaries. It is a fast track to burnout.

Because the work of shepherding can be messy, immature shepherds can become resentful if they perceive a lack of appreciation for their work. Finally, because shepherds bring stability and peace they can be overly fearful of risk which can lead to a lack of organizational momentum if they are in leadership positions.

Helpful Spiritual disciplines for shepherds include prioritizing pleasing God above all else, learning how to bring challenge and loving confrontation to others without fear. Shepherds must also deal with their own fears of being around other peoples pain. This requires growing self awareness and learning differentiation. Those involved in caring for others must be intentional in engaging in healthy 'self-care' (including having fun) and embracing their own limits. Finally, maturing shepherds must learn to step out of their own comfort zones for the sake of bringing momentum to those they are charged with leading.

Helping teachers mature

Finally, let's look at some common qualities that we regularly find in mature teachers. A master teacher brings understanding where there has been confusion. A good teacher is constantly learning and is not afraid to be challenged but rather values the opportunity to gain new insight. Teachers place high value on truth (especially scriptural truth) with is useful for training others in the ways of God.

Immature teachers can have potential blindspots. Some might settle for knowledge without understanding or wisdom (have you ever met a really smart fool?). Immature teachers can reject the 'spiritual & mystical' in favor of the 'observable-rational' and become overly skeptical as a result. This can manifest in a loss of wonder in learning and how we observe the world. Similarly a teacher who has unresolved fear can tend towards legalism and spiritual pride as a means of control and self-protection. This could even result in an irrational fear of being 'led astray' by new ideas.

Helpful Spiritual disciplines for teachers therefore could look like a developing a commitment to enacting scriptural truths through incarnation living, rather than just assenting to cognitive ideas. In addition, teachers can benefit from engaging in contemplative/ listening prayer which allows them to participate in the revelatory and mystical side of truth; this might also be achieved by engaging with creative arts and beauty, even something as simple as reading poetry which engages the heart as well as the mind. I love this quote from Robert Hugh Benson.

> *The heart is as divine a gift as the mind; and to neglect it in the search for God is to seek ruin.* (Robert Hugh Benson[43])

The ability to hold truth and mystery together in tension is a skill that takes intentionality to develop. Finally, teachers can be intentional in developing trust in the Holy Spirit who is the Spirit of truth, committed to leading us into all truth through prayer and faith.

May the Lord lead you into maturity.

Chapter 7: GIFTS FROM HOLY SPIRIT

"There are different kinds of gifts, but the same Spirit distributes them" (1 Corinthians 12.4 NIV)

The gifts of the Spirit have nothing to do with personal ambition or career orientation. They are not given to build individual reputations, to warrant superior positions in the local church, or to demonstrate spiritual advancement. They are not trophies, but tools - tools for touching and blessing others. (John Wimber[44])

In chapter four we considered how Holy Spirit is the gift of God. Holy Spirit is given to us as a downpayment guaranteeing our future inheritance, also as the spirit of adoption and as the spirit of truth. In each of these ways, Holy Spirit is leading us back to Jesus and the Father, inviting us deeper into the community that is our tri-une God.

How is it then that for many believers 'spiritual gifts' have become a turn off that push people away from God? Could it be that these gifts have not been faithfully stewarded to represent the Giver; that they have been misunderstood in such a way as to obscure the gift of God who is Holy Spirit?

Remember, it is important that we read Scripture in context. Paul wrote letters to specific communities experiencing specific issues at specific points in history. This context must not be ignored as we wrestle with what the Scriptures mean for us today. Let's take a look at the context of Paul's letter to the Corinthian church in which we find the final list of spiritual gifts.

De-Greeceing the Church

Corinth was a very strategic Greek city in the Roman empire acting as a kind of gateway for land movements between Italy and Asia Minor (modern day Turkey). It was a very successful commercial center with a much larger population than Athens. Because of the diverse trade routes that Corinth connected it's inhabitants came from all sorts of different cultures around the Roman Empire and beyond. As a result the city was also home to many pagan temples. Several historical sources report a high number of temple slaves and prostitutes working in the city.

Many of the pagan cults observed a form of dualism that elevated the value of spiritual knowledge and mystical experience above the physical and material world (including one's own flesh) which was considered to be of little or no value. Hence, not only was sexual immorality rife (e.g. temple prostitutes) in the city, but spiritual elitism (based on special knowledge or ecstatic experiences) was a common dynamic among the inhabitants of the city.

Paul had to address both of these cultural issues within the church at Corinth who, in keeping with their pagan roots, used their spiritual experiences, such as speaking in heavenly tongues or understanding spiritual mysteries (i.e. prophecy and revelation), to assert their own sense of significance and status within the church community. Paul was writing to a church that was no stranger to the very powerful spiritual atmosphere in Corinth but he was calling them out of their pagan Greek culture into the culture of the kingdom of God. The believers in Corinth needed some godly order to what they were doing in their corporate worship gatherings, not least by demonstrating proper care for the sick and poor amongst them. Part of their problem had been their spiritual pride and lack of concern for each other in the church community, hence he sandwiches the two chapters discussing spiritual gifts, chapters 12 & 14, around a whole chapter on how love needs to be at work amongst them in chapter 13. This over-emphasis on spiritual experience and under-emphasis on incarnational living can still be a problem in charismatic and pentecostal churches today.

Paul will seek to correct these wrong emphases by constantly calling the Corinthians back to their need to express *humility and unity* as a true foundation for their experiences of Holy Spirit (see 1 Cor 12.12-14).

The 'dancing hand' of the Spirit

Within this wider context Paul takes the opportunity to explain how the Holy Spirit is manifested in their gatherings through a variety of spiritual gifts.

> *"Now concerning spiritual things, brothers, I do not want you to be uninformed…"* (1 Cor 12:1 NET)

> *"There are different kinds of gifts, but the same Spirit distributes them. There are different kinds of service, but the same Lord. There are different kinds of working, but in all of them and in everyone it is the same God at work. Now to each one the manifestation of the Spirit is given for the common good. To one there*

is given through the Spirit a message of wisdom, to another a message of knowledge by means of the same Spirit, to another faith by the same Spirit, to another gifts of healing by that one Spirit, to another miraculous powers, to another prophecy, to another distinguishing between spirits, to another speaking in different kinds of tongues, and to still another the interpretation of tongues. All these are the work of one and the same Spirit, and he distributes them to each one, just as he determines." (1 Corinthians 12:4–11 <u>NIV</u>)

"Now you are the body of Christ, and each one of you is a part of it. And God has placed in the church first of all apostles, second prophets, third teachers, then miracles, then gifts of healing, of helping, of guidance, and of different kinds of tongues. Are all apostles? Are all prophets? Are all teachers? Do all work miracles? Do all have gifts of healing? Do all speak in tongues? Do all interpret? Now eagerly desire the greater gifts." (1 Corinthians 12:27–31 <u>NIV</u>)

It is worth noting that Paul uses a few different words before describing what we are calling 'gifts'. In his opening reference he uses a word that simply means 'spiritual'. There is no word that translates as 'gift' in 12.1. A better translation might be 'now concerning the things of the Spirit'. So Paul is changing topic from the previous discussion and wants now to focus on 'spiritual' things (e.g. the manifestation gifts) over and against speaking about practical and incarnational things that were the subject of the previous chapter (such as head coverings in worship gatherings and appropriate conduct at the Lord's supper).

Secondly, he precedes the list of gifts by referring to them firstly as varieties of 'gifts' (using a word that literally means 'freely distributed'); then as varieties of 'service' (or diverse ministries) and finally as varieties of 'activities' (or divine working). Each of these is a valid way for Paul to describe to the Corinthians what we have come to label simply as 'spiritual gifts'. So this passage is dealing with:-

    i.   <u>Distributed</u> gifts; same Spirit

    ii.   <u>Diverse</u> ministries; same Lord

    iii.   <u>Divine</u> workings; same God

Do you see how Paul is insisting that these varied gifts are trinitarian in origin? Despite the variation in how they look or are experienced, Paul is emphasizing that the Corinthians are experiencing the same Spirit, the same Lord and the same God. There is no elitism or hierarchy at play in these gifts. Don't misunderstand Paul. He is not suggesting a micro-separation in which the Spirit gives gifts, Jesus gives ministries and God gives workings... rather Paul is contending for the *unity* of these things all given by the triune God.

Paul then clarifies that the Spirit will manifest (or reveal) itself through each person for the benefit of *everyone*. Note therefore that *Holy Spirit determines the manifestation*, and is able to manifest divine activity through each person to bring benefit to all the people. Our word 'manifestation' comes from French and Latin origins meaning 'the festive hand' or 'dancing hand'; literally, the *dancing hand* of the Holy Spirit is embodied in all these different ways as people are empowered by the Spirit.

Paul then proceeds to list the following manifestations:

- utterance of wisdom,

- utterance of knowledge,

- faith,

- gifts of healing,

- working of miracles,

- prophecy,

- the ability to distinguish between spirits,

- various kinds of tongues,

- interpreting tongues

Paul emphasizes the first four gifts are each from the *same Spirit*. Unity is Paul's primary message here! Then in a follow up thought later in the same chapter Paul mentions,

- apostles,

- prophets,

- teachers,

- workers of miracles,

- healing,

- helping,

- administrating,

- various kinds of tongues.

Here Paul is emphasizing the diversity of the manifestations that should each be honored. Let's examine each one.

The utterance of wisdom

A message (or word) of wisdom is a revelatory gift. Paul refers to wisdom many times in this letter to the Corinthians, contrasting man's wisdom with God's wisdom and showing the spiritual source of these spiritual truths. This kind of wisdom is timely and insightful. It shines the light of kingdom understanding into the darkness of our earthly confusion.

There were entire religious and philosophical traditions that esteemed the concept of wisdom very highly, some coming from Jewish roots, others from Greek roots, and others still embedded in various forms of Gnosticism. Paul is referring to wisdom that comes from God the creator. In the book of Proverbs (chapters 8 and 9) a character called Wisdom is personified as being present at the creation of the Cosmos, working with the Lord. Of course, it is a metaphor, but it is showing that God created with wisdom embedded in the process.

King Solomon was renowned for his wisdom. We have the Book of Proverbs in the Old Testament. The opening verses tell us that Solomon's proverbs bring wisdom and instruction in righteousness, justice and equity, making wise the simple. Wisdom is not simply knowing principles or propositional truths, rather it is discerning which principles are relevant and how to apply them in different situations.

Wisdom is more than just guidance, but it can certainly help us understand how to act. I think the application of wisdom is that we live skillfully.

Wisdom can be profound in its simplicity. It can be direct yet nuanced. I often imagine that the Book of Proverbs was like King Solomon's ancient Twitter account... profound and pithy sayings loaded with understanding and wisdom. A message of wisdom does not necessarily have to be a short pithy proverb though. Under the anointing of the Holy Spirit a teacher might speak a message that brings wisdom to the body. Wisdom can be strategic and detailed, not just short and profound.

James the apostle tells us that if we lack wisdom we are to ask the Lord for it and he will give it to us generously (Jas 1.5). Wisdom and understanding are closely linked concepts. In fact, although we often say that Solomon asked for wisdom instead of riches, the Scriptures record that he actually asked for an understanding mind/ heart (1 Kings 3.9).

The utterance of knowledge

The word of knowledge is also a revelatory gift and has some potential overlap with the word of wisdom. Quite simply it is receiving knowledge spontaneously by means of the Holy Spirit. It seems to me that the knowledge Paul is referring to would be consistent with the knowledge that he has been speaking about to date in his letter to the Corinthians, where he has generally contrasted the folly of man's knowledge with the superior nature of God's knowledge.

In 1 Corinthians 2, Paul shows that only the Spirit of God can reveal the thoughts (mind) of God. This knowledge is therefore the revealing of God's thoughts brought by the Holy Spirit. It is not learned knowledge but revealed knowledge. I am grateful to those who value using our minds to worship God through learning and study, something that I feel is undervalued in many sections of the church. Diligent study yields knowledge that can be incredibly useful and fruitful. Paul himself was a Jewish scholar who studied under the one of the top Rabbis of his day. However, Paul is saying that there is a knowledge that cannot be learned, it can only be revealed. It is spiritual in nature and it comes from the Holy Spirit. But bear in mind, it differs from the 'secret' knowledge of the Gnostic mystery cults, in so far as it is freely given by the Spirit. This knowledge is not earned or given only to special initiates. Salvation does not come through 'special knowledge', but by grace through faith in Christ. Nor is this knowledge given for personal advancement, but for the benefit of the whole body.

These first two gifts (words of wisdom and words of knowledge) are revelatory in nature and are often considered useful for the purpose of instruction, teaching and leadership in the church, something that Paul is consistently committed to ensuring remains in line with his apostolic teaching. Remember that the Holy Spirit manifests on each person according to the grace of God, for the benefit of others. So I would encourage those who find themselves teaching in the church to be open to the Holy Spirit manifesting himself through these particular gifts.

A word of knowledge can also be an incredible way to reach out to those who do not yet know Christ. I was on a conference call this morning where someone shared a testimony about how they had shared a spontaneous word of knowledge with a worker in a large grocery store. This greatly encouraged the worker and opened them up to wanting to know more about Jesus. They ended up giving their life to Jesus. What the Christian didn't know was that the store worker had recently shared with their co-workers about their suicidal feelings. The word of knowledge ministered God's love to them and brought hope into their life.

Faith

According the writer of Hebrews, 'without faith it is impossible to please God' (Hebrews 11.6). We know that faith in Christ is the cornerstone of our salvation, through his grace (Ephesians 2.8). There is a longstanding scholarly debate about whether this saving faith is 'in Christ' or 'from Christ' (it's all about the Greek!). But here in his letter to the Corinthians, Paul is talking about a special manifestation of faith that comes as a grace gift. We often tell people that they need to *have* faith. In this instance, Holy Spirit *gives* faith as a grace gift.

In this context Paul is referring to a gift of faith that manifests through an increased measure of faith to see God work in a specific way, that was not present previously. The more we see God at work, the greater our expectation of God working becomes. So our faith grows, sometimes by seeing great breakthrough, other times by being tested in wilderness times. Here the spiritual manifestation of faith comes as a supernatural provision of faith itself.

I have received this gift on a couple of occasions when our church was confronted by a situation that required God to intervene and act miraculously. I was able to speak and encourage people with great confidence to put their trust in God to act because of the faith that I received as a gift from the Holy Spirit. I had no doubt in that moment that God would show up in power. It enabled our community to release bold prayer for God to act. Remember this gift is given for the good of the whole community, so it will usually need to be expressed and communicated in some way. It is unlikely to remain a private faith though it may need to be stewarded in personal prayer.

Faith requires us to act on it. The late John Wimber used to say that 'faith is spelled R-I-S-K'. But I think that that this kind of gift of faith means that there is little sense of risk in whatever endeavor it has been given for because it provides a strong sense of certainty that God will act. Faith is not presumptuous. It is initiated by God and it is centered in God. It is not faith in an outcome, but faith in God.

This kind of faith comes as a gift when the Holy Spirit is divinely at work amongst the members of Christ's body. Often it will release an atmosphere of strong expectation and even anticipatory celebration for what God is going to do, before he has done it. I wonder if this was what Paul and Silas experienced in the Philippian prison as they sang hymns and prayed while bound in their chains fully expectant that God would act to deliver them?

Gifts of healings

It is interesting to note that Paul refers to *gifts of healings* (in the plural). Supernatural (or divine) healing is simply the power of God at work to defeat sickness and brokenness and to restore wholeness to the person. It is quite clear in this passage that these healings are a grace gift from God.

Strangely, over the past century parts of the church have often welcomed the man or woman of God who moved in healing ministry, but it is only relatively recently that we have recovered the idea that anyone can be used to bring healing through this grace gift, since they are given a gift by God not a reward that they earned. I think of pioneers like John Wimber, Randy Clark and Che Ahn who not only moved in healing ministry themselves but have imparted this gift to many 'ordinary' people in the church to move in the Spirit's power through healing.

That God heals today is still not accepted by some parts of the church, especially by those in the more liberal stream who see the miracles and healings in Scripture as purely allegorical or even fictional. Paradoxically, parts of the conservative church believe that all of the miraculous gifts ceased at the completion of the writing and assembly of the canon of Scripture. Dr Randy Clark has written some excellent material on the theology of healing and he has written as a practitioner of divine healing.[45] He distinguishes between 'believing unbelievers' and 'unbelieving believers'! In other words, there are many outside the church who are very open to the idea that God can heal them, while there are still many in the church who have been taught not to believe in divine healing!

For many in the church who accept that God *can* heal today, their struggle is whether to believe he *will* heal and just what role the believer might have in the process. Around the world there are increasing numbers of believers who are being bold enough to take healing out onto the streets of their towns and cities so that their communities can experience God's goodness through this supernatural gift of healing that God releases.

The apostle Paul points out that these healings are a gift of grace from God and they are a manifestation of the Spirit working through his people (not just healing his people, but working through his people healing the sick!). while I would not make too rigid a point I think it is sage advice to consider that when we gather and pray for healing, we should anticipate a plurality of healing encounters to happen. It is in God's nature to give life and Jesus own mission was to heal the sick. Paul gives no guidance as to what template of prayers might be offered. He says nothing here of whether there is to be laying on of hands, or prayers offered to God, or whether healing declarations are to be made. There are other Scriptures that might help us develop such models of praying for healing, but that is not his goal in this letter. Rather Paul is validating that the gifts of healing are from the Holy Spirit for the service of his people. This healing might be of the body, the emotions or even of the spirit (e.g. deliverance from oppressive spirits). We are whole beings and God's healing ministers to our whole being too.

Just as a side note, I think it is very important that we do not elevate this form of healing by the Spirit above other more natural and medical forms of healing that God has given us. Paul Manwaring has written an excellent book called 'Kisses from a Good God' which goes some way to address this issue and records his own journey of healing from cancer through surgery. I am always in admiration for the child-like faith of people who persevere in prayer for healing, but I also get concerned as a Pastor trying to care for people who will not seek medical care as part of their healing journey. Even the Apostle Paul encouraged his spiritual son Timothy to 'take a little wine' for his ailments and stomach issues (1 Tim 5.23) and he also showed deep respect for Dr Luke who was a physician (see Colossians 4.14). We have each been given a physical body which we must value and care for out of respect to God (to say nothing of our own health). To solely rely on the Holy Spirit to care for our body shows a tragic lack of responsibility and stewardship on our own part and is theologically irresponsible as we slide towards a dualistic approach that values spiritual things over physical things. This is why the theology of the Incarnation, Jesus becoming flesh, is so important for the charismatic and pentecostal churches to embrace. Yes, God is gracious to heal divinely (I am utterly convinced of that) but we must also be proactive in stewarding our own health.

The following extract is from the Jewish wisdom book of Sirach[46] (also known as Ecclesiasticus or the Wisdom of Ben Sira) and was written around 200 BC.

> *"Honor physicians for their services, for the Lord created them; for their gift of healing comes from the Most High, and they are rewarded by the king. The skill of physicians makes them distinguished, and in the presence of the great they are admired. The Lord created medicines out of the earth, and the sensible will not despise them. Was not water made sweet with a tree in order that its power might be known? And he gave skill to human beings that he might be glorified in his marvelous works. By them the physician heals and takes away pain; the pharmacist makes a mixture from them. God's works will never be finished; and from him health spreads over all the earth. My child, when you are ill, do not delay, but pray to the Lord, and he will heal you. Give up your faults and direct your hands rightly, and cleanse your heart from all sin. Offer a sweet-smelling sacrifice, and a memorial portion of choice flour, and pour oil on your offering, as much as you can afford. Then give the physician his place, for the Lord created him; do not let him leave you, for you need him. There may come a time when recovery lies in the hands of physicians, for they too pray to the Lord that he grant them success in diagnosis and in healing, for the sake of preserving life. He who sins against his Maker, will be defiant toward the physician."* (Sirach 38:1–15 NRSV)

Thank God for physicians and pharmacists!

Working of miracles

The Greek words which translate as "working of miracles" give us our English words *energized* and *dynamite*! Miracles are simply the power of God on display and interestingly Paul differentiates them from the gifts of healings. while all the gifts are God's grace at work, they are to be distinguished from the power encounters experienced through miracles.

When Paul went to Ephesus he saw 'extraordinary' miracles take place there, particularly in relation to the powerful occult and magic practices that took place there (Acts 19.11-12). This miraculous power ministry is often (but not exclusively) demonstrated as the Kingdom of God is proclaimed in places where dark powers have strongholds. It reflects the overcoming power of the Kingdom of God in the confrontation against the counterfeit power of demonic and occult activity.

There is really no constraint nor description given here as to how God's power might be displayed. Aside from healings, I have witnessed several miracles, including a person receiving gold teeth, a leg growing by an inch and weather patterns changing over a very specific local area. I have heard first hand testimonies of miraculous provision, food multiplication, divine favor and even miraculous protection from harm. Paul experienced a miraculous earthquake that freed him from a jail. Jesus walked on water and turned water into wine.

These miracles are a manifestation of the Spirit's dynamic power for the service of God's people given by his grace.

In our modern scientific age of skepticism, it is common for people both outside and inside the church to doubt the veracity of miracle claims. Today the Catholic Church has an incredibly rigorous set of criteria for categorizing something as a miracle. Certainly, there can be false claims of miracles (either naively or worse still, deceptively), aimed at grabbing attention but at the end of the day because a miracle is a supernatural encounter that cannot be explained naturally or scientifically, we have to exercise faith or at the very least, be willing to suspend our unbelief.

A miracle testimony should neither be exaggerated nor downplayed. We must learn to simply report things as they are in order to honor God's work amongst his people. We must neither fall into the trap of denying miracles, nor of relying on miracles when God has actually called us to act as his instrument. Once again, this whole passage is based on the premise that the Spirit works through God's people. That is not the issue. Remember Paul is addressing spiritual pride and arrogance in the Corinthian church community with a view to restoring a culture of unity and communal care.

When God does a miracle then only God should receive the glory for it. Jesus cautioned his disciples that on the last day God will reject many who claimed to do miracles in his name. Miracles are a sign not a spectacle, they are for breakthrough not for entertainment. They should point to God not to a person.

Prophecy revisited

We have already reviewed "the one who prophesies" in our look at Romans 12 and the prophet (people as gift) in Ephesians 4. Simply to say in this passage, Paul is telling his readers that prophecy is a manifestation of God's Spirit by means of God bringing His timely revelation concerning his purposes to strengthen, encourage and comfort the body (1 Cor 14.2) This should not be taken to imply that someone who receives this manifestation is necessarily a 'prophet', rather that the 'dancing hand[47]' of the Holy Spirit is graciously empowering an individual for service with this gift. Authentic Holy Spirit prophesy will build up the body not tear it down or elevate the speaker (1 Cor 14.4).

Distinguishing between spirits

This is the God-given ability to distinguish between spirits, i.e. to discern the source of spiritual power, revelation or activity. Typically, this is discerning between what is of the Holy Spirit (including heavenly angelic activity), what is of the flesh (i.e. man made), and what is demonic/satanic/antichrist in nature.

Jesus said that we would know [false] prophets by their fruit (Matt 7.15-16). For as long as there have been prophets there have been those who prophesy out of their own flesh for personal gain or worse, from their occult practices. Ultimately the Holy Spirit produces good fruit! It is vital that the church can discern the source of prophetic utterances.

This gift is not simply for judging prophecy. Given that all these gifts listed in 1 Corinthians 12 are forms of manifestations of the Holy Spirit, this gift will help us discern what is behind the spiritual activity we observe.

During the spiritual renewal and outpouring in Toronto during the 1990's there was much controversy about some of the manifestations that were exhibited. There were reports of people making strange animal noises, shaking, falling over, rolling on the floor and laughing hysterically. John Arnott led the Catch the Fire church in Toronto through this renewal and helpfully writes, "*sometimes, even the powerful shaking is not because the Holy Spirit is deliberately shaking them, but rather they are reacting to His power and presence... keeping our eyes on the manifestations themselves is not the correct response. The manifestations are only the outward part of the Holy Spirit's work – the inner work is what's important".*[48]

I remember travelling on a mission trip to India several years ago. During one of our worship times, a local lady was rolling on the floor quite violently from side to side for about 20 minutes. Several people were very concerned by this, but we encouraged them to let God work. They were correctly discerning the presence of a demonic spirit. However, the lady was actually encountering the Holy Spirit in a powerful way and the demonic spirit was leaving her. Had we tried to 'shut down' what was happening we may well have interfered with the wonderful deliverance God was doing.

On other occasions the gift of discernment can enable you to know whether to bring a word of correction or mercy to a brother or sister who is acting out of their flesh or woundedness. Imagine if a child stood on a sharp nail and was screaming and hopping around the house. Do you chastise them for being disruptive or do you discern that they are in pain and need to experience healing and care? Discernment is vital and an invaluable gift for shepherds to operate in.

I agree with Dr Mark Stibbe who writes that *"the gift of discernment is one of the most marginalized and yet one of the most vital gifts for the body of Christ today. We undervalue it to our great peril."*[49]

Tongues and Interpretations

There is something of a mystery that still surrounds this particular manifestation of the Holy Spirit for many people. Speaking in different 'tongues' or 'languages' is mentioned in a few different New Testament passages, but it would be wise to allow what Paul writes elsewhere in his letter to the Corinthians to direct our understanding for his use here in chapter 12. Broadly, it can apply not only to the speech organ (the tongue), but to the utterance of speech (e.g. a human language or ecstatic speech). In chapter 13, Paul mentions speaking in the tongues of men (human languages) and angels (presumably an ecstatic unrecognizable speech), but in context he is challenging his readers that without the motivation of love, neither is of any value.

Then in chapter 14, Paul speaks in some detail about how this manifestation should be administrated, its proper value and its purpose in the communal worship setting. From this exposition, it seems clear that Paul is not telling the Corinthians about speaking in recognizable human languages (which is the clear inference in the Pentecost tongues in Acts 2.6), rather he is referring to ecstatic and unrecognizable speech.

Such unrecognizable speech is directed toward God not men (1 Cor 14.2); others will not understand such speech for it is a spiritual mystery; while it may edify the speaker it has little value to others, certainly, less value than prophecy which builds up the hearers (1 Cor 14.4). While speaking in tongues is a legitimate manifestation of the Spirit, it should not be considered on a par with prophecy unless, through interpretation, others in the church may be built up . Therefore we should see that tongues (at least in this passage) is a personal prayer language to God that is of benefit to the individual, but of little value to the wider community.

Paul seems to imply that if a tongue is interpreted (another manifestation from the same Spirit) it might communicate revelation, knowledge, prophecy or teaching (1 Cor 14.6), and that it is better that the one speaking in tongues prays for an interpretation in order to benefit others.

I remember an occasion when I was praying with the leadership team of my church. We were asking God for wisdom for a particular situation and I felt a very strong urge to pray out in tongues, not quite knowing how to pray in my own words. I asked permission from the team (since tongues would usually be a personal prayer language). After I had prayed, one of the other leaders received an interpretation to my prayer which helped us in discerning how to pray further and how the Spirit was leading us.

Keep in mind that Paul's whole letter to the Corinthians is dealing with how they might bring unity amongst their community in the face of frequent prideful and self-centered actions and behavior. Paul's tone on speaking in tongues is therefore filtered through this lens. He is hardly 'putting down' this manifestation of the Spirit as having no value, rather he is recognizing that in the context of the Corinthian church and their divisive problems, there is a more noble way to receive and utilize such a gift for the greater good of the community.

In classical Pentecostal theology, speaking in tongues is considered the definitive sign of being filled with Holy Spirit, however the Scriptures do not support this view. Yes, for some it is the evidence. But we also read of others prophesying or receiving boldness when they are filled with Holy Spirit. The manifestations of the Spirit are varied… but from the same Spirit.

Interlude #1: all these are empowered by one and the same Spirit, who apportions to each one individually as he wills

It is worth re-iterating the contents of verse 11 which echo the opening verses of this same chapter. These manifestations are empowered by the Holy Spirit who gives himself to individuals in the manner that the Holy Spirit desires. We can eagerly ask for the Holy Spirit to manifest among his people through these gifts, but the Spirit is always the one who decides how to work and through whom. This implies that we do not get to decide what our gifts our, but instead that we discover how the Holy Spirit is gracing us.

The Holy Spirit is the gift from God (Acts 2.38), something which the Corinthians seemed to have lost sight of.

Interlude #2: Are some gifts better than others?

> *"Now you are the body of Christ, and each one of you is a part of it. And God has placed in the church first of all apostles, second prophets, third teachers, then miracles, then gifts of healing, of helping, of guidance, and of different kinds of tongues. Are all apostles? Are all prophets? Are all teachers? Do all work miracles? Do all have gifts of healing? Do all speak in tongues? Do all interpret?"* (1 Corinthians 12:27–30 NIV)

At the close of 1 Corinthians 12 Paul seems to re-iterate certain gifts and also include some new gifts not previously mentioned . At first reading one might think that he is ranking the gifts, but this seems to fly in the face of everything he has been trying to communicate in the chapter to date. Instead of some gifts having more importance than others, and hence, some parts of the body being deemed less honorable, Paul has just stated that the parts of the body that appear weaker are in fact indispensable and parts of the body that we think are less honorable, are in fact worthy of us bestowing greater honor to (1 Cor 12.22-24).

Rather, it seems to make better sense to understand that there is a divine order to things. Paul lists apostles, prophets and teachers but it is unclear whether he is now considering these to be spiritual manifestations as in the early part of the chapter (c.f. the people-as-gifts idea in Ephesians 4.11).

So when Paul orders these gifts as 'first, second, third, then...' several scholarly greek lexicons and dictionaries all translate these adverbs 'firstly, secondly, thirdly' to describe a sequential list, rather than a hierarchy. This makes sense given the repeated use of the word 'then', meaning 'subsequent in the list' and also Paul's overwhelming critique on the elitism of the Corinthians.

Let me illustrate. In Ephesians 2.20, Paul uses the picture of building foundations to describe the ministry of the apostles and prophets. As a former structural engineer, I can tell you that the first thing you construct on any building is the foundations. Some of the most spectacular buildings ever erected would not be possible if it were not for their foundations. In this sense, the foundations have prime importance, because without them the remainder of the building is doomed to be unstable and weak. If foundations are not attended to properly at the outset what follows is at risk of catastrophic collapse. However, I don't know anyone who looks at a building and admires its foundations. Rather they look at the lines and roof form, or the way the building design serves its occupants effectively. Foundations must go in first, but they are not the main purpose of the building.

I think Paul's list in 12.28 is rather like an order of construction for the body. First apostles, second prophets, third teachers then 'works of power'; without these ministries laying the foundations, everything that follows is prone to misalignment and instability. For Paul, that will mean the apostolic witness of the Gospel and it's sound teaching lies at the forefront of making the church healthy. That would explain why Paul was so dedicated to his apostolic ministry to the churches he planted, because he knew that he had to lay a solid foundation if they were to last and to grow (see Romans 15.20 & 1 Cor 3.10-14).

Subsequent to these four foundational ministries are other gifts of the Spirit. Paul reiterates healing and tongues, but also adds in helping and guiding (administrating) which have not been mentioned before (and are not mentioned again elsewhere).

Helping

Helping is literally the ability to assist and aid others. It is the only time this particular word is used in the New Testament. Can you imagine any church functioning successfully without this spiritual ministry in operation? I wonder if Paul threw this into his list to illustrate his earlier point about what we deem weaker actually being indispensable! Can you imagine crowds of Christians flocking to a meeting with a special guest minister who was renowned for the gift of helpfulness... no? Perhaps Paul still wants to challenge our perceptions of these gifts today?

An example of the need for this 'helpfulness' would be in Acts 6.1 when the Hellenist widows where being neglected in the daily distribution of food. The Apostles then identified seven men who could oversee the meeting of this need, while they committed themselves to their apostolic ministry of prayer and preaching. The seven men came to the aid and assistance of the needy in the community, operating as helpers.

I can think of several people in our church who clearly operate in this gift. They have a peculiar grace to assist people in moments when others either don't see the need or perhaps when others don't know how to help. These people are incredible gifts to the church and are a real blessing to our community. Perhaps you know someone like that? That could well be the Holy Spirit manifesting his grace through helpfulness.

The Holy Spirit operates as our helper. How fitting of the Spirit then to manifest in us through embodied helpfulness.

Guiding/ Administration

The gift of guiding (NIV)/ administrating (ESV) is actually from a greek word whose root meaning is 'to steer'. It is a leadership gift that brings wise direction to the community. We commonly describe people who are highly organized as good administrators, or we create 'administrative' job roles that describe support functions that release leaders to lead, but this really isn't what Paul is talking about.

The biblical ministry of administrating is a directional and leadership gift (of course, it helps if you are highly organized). In this case, the NIV seems to be the better translation using the word 'guiding'. A ship is powered by the wind or an engine but is steered by a rudder. The gift of guiding is like the rudder. It may not provide momentum, but it does provide direction and sets the course.

The church desperately needs people who can operate in this divinely given ministry gift. Remember, the church is not called to be a static organization, but rather a dynamic and mobile community following the leading of the Holy Spirit in the mission of God. Spirit led guidance is therefore vital if the church is to be effective in it's mission and purpose.

Several greek lexicons include the English word 'governing' as a definition. I have steered away from using that (pun intended), since I think we tend to default to associate a degree of hierarchal heavy-handedness to that word that I do not think is intended by the root concept of steering and direction. Guiding is for the benefit of the whole vessel.

Other New Testament gifts

---

1 Corinthians 7.7

> *"I wish that all were as I myself am. But each has his own gift from God, one of one kind and one of another"* (1 Cor 7:7)

The context of this passage is a discussion on marriage, singleness and abstaining from sexual relations within marriage. while this passage does not explicitly specify a particular gift, it does affirm that each person (single or married) has a unique gifting. Paul probably is referring to his own *gift of celibacy* given the context. He is emphasizing that God gives the gifts to each person as He sees fit and we therefore are recipients of different gifts. To this end, it can also be assumed that *the grace to be married* is also a legitimate alternative gift. As someone who regularly does pre-marital counseling this is a much overlooked verse. There is much pressure from within the church to be married. For centuries, the church considered singleness (celibacy) to be a higher spiritual calling than marriage. It seems that the pendulum has now swung in the opposite direction, and most churches see single people as 'candidates' for marriage. In reality, Paul is saying, both singleness and marriage are a grace gift from the Lord. It is important to discern the Lord's leading rather than just be led by the desires of our flesh.

We are not to compare ourselves to others, but we are to recognize and receive our diversity of giftedness. Comparison is perhaps one of the greatest barriers to building a healthy church community. Paul seemed acutely aware of this and so repeatedly tells his readers to honor each other and prefer each other so that they might not fall into the trap of comparison which leads to pride and envy.

Ephesians 3:7

"Of this gospel I was made a minister according to the gift of God's grace, which was given me by the working of his power" (Ephesians 3.7)

Again, Paul's emphasis here is that our gifts are an expression of God's grace, given by the power of God at work in us. It seems that Paul is revealing that his role as a servant of the Gospel was empowered by God's grace gift to him. The gift is God's grace. The fruit of that grace is Paul's powerful ministry of declaring the Gospel.

1 Peter 4.10-11

"Show hospitality to one another without grumbling. As each has received a gift, use it to serve one another, as good stewards of God's varied grace: whoever speaks, as one who speaks oracles of God; whoever serves, as one who serves by the strength that God supplies—in order that in everything God may be glorified through Jesus Christ. To him belong glory and dominion forever and ever. Amen" (1 Peter 4:9-11)

Peter is identifying that *each* person has received a gift, noting the the wide distribution and diversity as Paul did. One of the purposes of our receiving gifts from God is to use them to serve one another. This is what appropriate stewardship of our gift looks like. Just as the gift is an expression of God's grace towards us, He intends it to be given as an expression of His grace to others. Our gifts are not to be collected or hoarded like some trophy cabinet. Nor are they given for us to feel validated or smug! They are given so that we can serve someone else to the glory of God, hence "whoever speaks [should speak] as one who speaks oracles of God". The gift should clearly demonstrate its source is in God's grace and should be stewarded with the reverence befitting of representing God.

It seems that there may be three different gifts in view for Peter; *showing hospitality* (v 9); *speaking oracles of God* (v11a); *serving* (v11b - probably with servant leadership in mind).

Paul is also clear that the goal of our using spiritual gifts is so that God would be glorified through Jesus Christ.

Hebrews 2.4

"God also testified to it by signs, wonders and various miracles, and by gifts of the Holy Spirit distributed according to his will." (Heb 2.4 NIV)

The unknown author of Hebrews is commenting on the authenticity of the Gospel message that they are proclaiming as testified to by signs, wonders and various miracles. Most English translations use the word 'gifts' in this verse, but there is no specific word for this in the Greek, rather the idea is connected to the word 'distributed'. What is being distributed? Well it could be *the signs, wonders and various mir-*

acles, (c.f. *miracles* in 1 Cor 12) or it could *the Holy Spirit* who is the gift of God (c.f. Acts 2.38). Again, the climax of this thought is that God distributes the gift according to his will.

Wrapping up the gifts from the Spirit

Perhaps you've heard the expression, 'I can't see the wood for the trees'! It usually means that we are looking so closely at something, we forget to zoom out and see the bigger picture.

We must not lose sight of the context for receiving and using spiritual gifts. Here is my list of the top six basic things to remember so that we keep gifts in their proper context and do not become distracted or obsessed by something that is not 'the main thing'!

1) Holy Spirit is <u>THE</u> gift of God. On the day of Pentecost Peter tells his listeners "Repent and be baptized everyone of you in the name of Jesus Christ for the forgiveness of your sins, and *you will receive the gift of the Holy Spirit*. For the promise is for you and for your children and for all who are far off, everyone whom the Lord our God calls to himself" (Acts 2.38-39). We later discover that even the Gentiles received "*the gift of the Holy Spirit*". God gives Holy Spirit as <u>the</u> gift to all who believe on the name of Jesus Christ. Don't substitute THE GIFT for the gifts!

2) Spiritual gifts are *gifts*! (were you expecting something more profound?). Gifts are not earned; they are given by a generous Giver! They are not badges of honor or status! Please stop pretending that you somehow earned your gift or that somehow you cashed in more

of your faith for your gift than the person next to you. Remember even your measure of faith was given to you by God (Romans 12.3).

3) *All* spiritual gifts are gifts! (I told you this wasn't profound!). Yes, Paul tells the Corinthians to eagerly desire prophecy and he wishes that they might all speak in tongues, but we are to rejoice at ALL the gifts that God has given to the church, not simply those we think are more spectacular than others. Paul specifically reminds the Corinthians that all the body members are valuable, so we should not despise certain gifts below others. Let's take a reality check for a moment. Do you honestly think that the gift of working miracles is more valuable than the gift of administration? Or what about the gift of healings compared to the gift of helps? Or is the gift of teaching more important than the gift of generosity? Sure, some gifts are outwardly more 'impressive' or 'miraculous' but most communities will soon cease to be healthy if the gifts of helps, generosity and administration are not released and celebrated! Let's recognize and honor all the gifts and stop exalting some over others.

4) Spiritual gifts are given *as a blessing for the body*. If a gift becomes self-indulgent and self-serving then it is no longer a blessing to the body and it is being misused (Paul has to correct the Corinthian church on this precise issue). If I am the recipient of God's grace i.e. a spiritual gift, then it has been given to me so that I might bless others! This is a value at the very heart of the Kingdom of Heaven, "It is more blessed to give than to receive" (Acts 19.35). Think how immature children can become overly protective of a toy they have been given. Our heavenly Father is lovingly asking his children to 'share nicely' what he has given us!

5) The fertile soil into which spiritual gifts are to be sown is LOVE. Sandwiched in between two chapters on spiritual gifts, Paul takes an-

other whole chapter to tell the Corinthian churches that to use the spiritual gifts without demonstrating LOVE for others is a fruitless endeavor (1 Cor 13). Love cannot be separated from exercising these gifts! This is not meant to diminish our eagerness for gifts rather to increase our desire to imitate Christ's love when we use gifts. After all, Jesus told his disciples that the way they demonstrate love for each other that would be the sign that they were his followers, not their spectacular use of gifts (John 13.34-35). Paul sums it up nicely with the statement "pursue love and earnestly desire the spiritual gifts" (1 Cor 14.1). It amuses me that 1 Corinthians 13 is often read at weddings, when it was actually written to address a dysfunctional charismatic congregation! As 'gift-toting' charismatics, many of us would do well to meditate long and hard on the 'love chapter' asking the Holy Spirit for a deeper revelation of what it looks like to love others as we put our spiritual gifts to use in the service of others. We are called to walk in the power of love and avoid the love of power. Power corrupts. The apostle James captures this in his Epistle. "For where you have envy and selfish ambition, there you find disorder and every evil practice." (James 3:16 NIV).

6) Finally, spiritual gifts are *not* the goal, they are a means to an end! Ephesians 4.8 paints a healthy perspective on the giving of gifts. In giving gifts to men, Jesus demonstrates his benevolence towards those he has taken 'captive', as well as revealing his abundant resources from which the gifts derive. Spiritual gifts should ultimately lead the church into a greater sense of submission to Christ, serving Christ and being captivated in our worship of Christ. "… *use [them] to serve one another, as good stewards of God's varied grace…in order that in everything God may be glorified through Jesus Christ. To him belong glory and dominion forever and ever. Amen"* (1 Peter 4.10-11).

They really are all about God and not about us. That is the effect that their use should have, to redirect our focus toward God and away from ourselves.

Purpose revisited

The passages that we explored indicate that spiritual gifts are given for a variety of reasons. Here are a few that I see revealed in these texts.

i.   They are given as varied expressions of God's *grace* (1 Peter 4:10), in other words they are manifestations of God's *power* at work among us. This gives us the ability to minister and operate beyond our own ability as we embody God's power at work in us and through us.

ii.   They are given to build up *unity* within the body and *mature* us to achieve the stature of the fullness of Christ (Ephesians 4.13). When I hear stories of how congregations and communities has been divided over the use of gifts, I can't help but suspect that it is the way they have been used that is the issue, not the presence of the gifts themselves. As I mentioned earlier, *the way gifts are used is of utmost importance to the Apostle Paul*. We are to exhibit Christ-likeness in exercising the gifts out of a motivation of love, faith and service.

iii.   They are given to reflect and serve the *diversity* of the roles each part of the body has to play in loving one another (Romans 12.4-5). The body of Christ is diverse and that is cause for celebration! Likewise, the gifts are diverse. We should celebrate that fact and not project our own gifts onto other people. Dr C Peter Wagner refers to this problem as 'gift projection', when we think other people ought to operate in the same gifts as we do. When we take this attitude we cease to honor the diversity Christ created in the body.

iv. They are given for the *common good,* i.e. they are given to bless many people (1 Cor 12.7). I am always blessed when I recognize God's gifts in action, even if I am not the immediate recipient of grace through the gift. It speaks to me of God at work, building up his body. It is important that we can celebrate what Holy Spirit is doing amongst the body especially when we are not directly involved as agent or recipient. When the body is built up we all benefit.

v. Certain gifts are given as a sign to believers and some for unbelievers all with the purpose of *revealing* Christ (1 Cor 14.24-25).

It appears that gifts are always intended to have an impact beyond the person exercising them. In other words, once we receive a gift from God, we now become the custodians of a gift to be given away to bless others. By becoming a giver we bear the image of our Maker.

Can I ask for specific gifts?

This is an interesting question to ponder. I think that you can have confidence to go before our loving heavenly Father and to ask for what you need in order to accomplish the good works he has prepared in advance for you. James tells us that we do not have because we do not ask, and then immediately warns us that we are inclined to ask with the wrong motivation. I think therefore we can trust in Father God's generosity but we balance that with keeping our motives pure (James 4.2-5).

In my own life I asked for the gift of prophecy quite early on after discovering the gifts of the spirit and have then stewarded and cultivated this gift with time. As I have grown in this gift what excites me most is not whether my prophetic words are impressive or detailed but that I get to encourage and build up the body. I can't tell you how many times I have given what felt to me like a 'weak' or unimpressive word only to find that it released hope and encouragement to the recipient in ways that I could never have imagined. I always end up being encouraged at the way God works through me (and often in spite of me) to build up the body.

During my time serving as a lay elder in a congregational church in the UK, I consciously asked for the gift of guiding (administration) and the gift of wisdom. They seemed to be gifts that I needed in that season to equip me to do the work that God had called me to. Perhaps he would have given them to me anyway, but by being intentional about asking for these gifts I was acknowledging my particular call to service in that season.

Since I have been serving full time on a pastoral team in a much larger church here in the USA, I ask for wisdom and discernment to know how God has gifted the body here, (knowing that I am not called to be everything to everyone), and to grow in my teaching gift. I have the privilege to serve people who have their own international ministries and are incredibly gifted in their particular calling. They are gifts to the body. My job is to serve them (which is a grace gift in itself).

When I first joined the staff team at church, truthfully I was a little overwhelmed for the first few months. We have so many wonderful, gifted people in our church that I was overwhelmed at times figuring out how I could possibly lead such capable people. After several months, the Lord lovingly rebuked me and reminded me that I was called to *serve* them not 'lead' them (at least, not in the way I was envisioning 'leading'; I now see that this is the 'serving' that the apostle Peter writes about in 1 Pet 4.10-11). We already have a wonderful apostolic leader in our church. My role is to serve and love this community and equip them to be fruitful in the calling that God has placed on their lives. Of course, I am called to be a leader but it is through *servant leadership*. The Apostle Paul modeled servant leadership through the way he invested in the churches he planted and oversaw. He acted as a spiritual father to them.

Jesus himself modeled the kind of servant leadership that he called his disciples to. He powerfully demonstrated his humble servant heart by washing the feet of his disciples.

May the body of Christ be clothed in His humility as we put our gifts at the service of others.

The issue of stewardship

You might wonder why we even need to identify our gifts. Why not just trust that we will have what we need when we need it? There is something to be said for the simplicity and faith of this approach! However, I'd like to suggest that we ought to identify our gifts for three good reasons.

Firstly, I believe that we will be held to account for what we have done with what we have been given. Jesus told parables implying this. Accountability begins with an honest assessment of what we have been given and recognizing who gave it to us. It is a question of _stewardship_. Will we be faithful with little so that we might be trusted with more?

Secondly, I believe that most gifts require us to grow in their use in order to become mature in how we use them. For example, imagine that I have been given a new tennis racquet for Christmas. I can be very grateful and show it to all my family and friends rejoicing that I am now the owner of a new tennis racquet. However, a tennis racquet has a specific function, which is to hit a tennis ball in a game of tennis (and possibly to double as an air guitar in the off season!). The likelihood is that I can swing my tennis racquet around quite easily, but unless I practice with it I am unlikely to become proficient at hitting tennis balls with it and accomplish the kind of tennis shots that more experienced tennis players can. So it is with my spiritual gift. Some of the gifts need to be used, explored, tested, practiced with until I become used to operating with them. It is a question of _maturity_.

A good example is the gift of prophecy. Most people I know who exercise this gift have learned how to steward it through practice and testing, trial and error (in a safe environment where mistakes can be learning opportunities... small groups are great incubators for growing in gifts). When we are given a gift, it is given in accordance to the measure of our faith. As our faith grows (which it should do over time), so our gift and our competency in our gift should also be growing.

Finally, since gifts are given so that we can bless others, I need to know what I have been equipped with so that I can know how best to be a blessing to others in the body, knowing where I fit within the body. How can I give away what I don't know I have? It is a question of _generosity_. When we know how God likes to operate through us and manifest his grace, we can better spot the opportunities to see him work through us in this way. If I know my gift is an opportunity to exhibit generosity, then I will become sensitive to spotting opportunities to represent the Father's generosity through my gift. If God has given me the gifts of healing, then I learn to be on the look out for people who need to receive the healing touch of God. If I see people who are struggling, then I get to use my gift of encouragement. You get the picture. It is more blessed to give than to receive!

Discovering how you have been gifted

So here's the bottom line. If you want to figure out what your gifts are then the chances are you will need to start serving other people. Now I don't believe that this has to be limited within the four walls of church meetings, but certainly given that the gifts are given to build up the body, it seems that serving and loving the body is the context for many of these discoveries.

In short, don't wait to discover your gifts before you start serving. Start serving so that you can discover your gifts! You will probably need to serve in different ways, maybe even among different groups of people. I discovered what were my gifts (and what weren't my gifts!) by serving in youth ministry for a time, then as a small group leader, then by serving on a worship team, then on prayer teams etc. It was a journey of discovery over several years. Once I had discovered my areas of giftedness, I only grew in maturity as I used them and stewarded them according the measure of faith that I was growing into. To this day I frequently have to exercise faith when using my gifts, not because I don't believe I'm gifted, but because I rarely *feel* gifted. There is a difference between confidence and complacency. We are called to live by faith, not by feelings! Without faith it is impossible to please God (Hebrews 11.6).

If you are not serving somewhere, then find a need and fill it! It may not be your 'calling', but it is the means through which God can refine both your gifting and character.

There are many different online surveys and questionnaires available to help you discern your spiritual gifts. Some are free, some are not. While gift surveys and questionnaires can be helpful they do not fix your giftedness. They are simply a man-made means of helping identify actions, behaviors and motivations that might indicate your spiritual gifts. You can rejoice knowing that it is your generous, gift-giving Heavenly Father who loves you, who determines your giftedness!

The best indication that you operate in a particular gift is the witness of those around you who can see and affirm your gifting. Most questionnaires therefore assume that you have some 'ministry' experience i.e. that you put yourself in an environment where gifts can be demonstrated and seen by others.

Have a go at taking a survey. Just search the Internet for something like 'spiritual gifts survey' and you'll be surprised how many resources are available. Of course, they will all have their own slightly unique take on each gift. Share the results with someone you trust who knows you. What surprises you? What do you find encouraging? What questions does it raise for you?

AFTERWORD

'Love releases us for taking one more risk than we might dare;

glory breaks through dark and danger, shows the Lord trans-
figured there.

God who planted our affections, help your gifts to grow more
free,

fan in us the fires of loving, daring, dancing Trinity'

(Michael Hare Duke)

Given the incredible growth of the global charismatic movement and the church renewal movement of the last sixty
years it seems that the Holy Spirit continues to breathe on
the church and awaken her to these gifts. Why then do so many
Christians still not know what their spiritual gifts are or know 'how'
to grow in using them? Why do we have churches that are happy to
say that they believe in the spiritual gifts but neither have an authentic expression of them nor have any means of incorporating training
in the spiritual gifts as part of daily discipleship? I suspect the answer
is that because of a few negative experiences the 'baby was thrown
out with the bath water'! And why do some churches allow selfishness and pride to go unchallenged when it comes to spiritual gifts being misused? I suspect it comes from a misunderstanding of the nature of spiritual power. This is such a shame considering that we are
taking about fundamentally good gifts from a good Father meant for

the benefit and unity of the whole Church.

If you have been hurt by the misuse of spiritual gifts or over mis-un-derstandings related to spiritual gifts I want to compassionately urge you to ask God to restore what has been stolen from you and invite him to bring healing to any wounded-ness you have experienced. I am convinced that spiritual gifts are a vital means of God's grace equipping you to fulfill his calling on your life and your role in the mission of his church. As a church Pastor I am grieved by the hurt you have experienced. It breaks my heart.

A good place to start is simply to ask the Lord to reveal to you if there is someone that you need to forgive for contributing to your fear or mis-trust of spiritual gifts. Then, by God's grace, pray something like "Heavenly Father, as an act of my will I choose to forgive (*name*) for (*what they did*). I give them a gift of my forgiveness. I let go of any bitterness or judgment I have held towards them. I give up my right to sit in judgment over them and I trust that you are a merciful and just Judge. Now forgive me for partnering with any lies I have be-lieved about you and your good gifts (*ask the Lord to reveal what lies you have believed about spiritual gifts, and then ask him to show you what His truth is*). Please heal my wounded heart. I gladly receive the gifts you have given me, trusting that you are a good Father and these gifts are given as a blessing. Amen".

Remember, we walk by faith not by feelings. Sometimes we have to act in faith and allow God to bring his healing to our emotions in due time.

A closing blessing

May you walk in the overflow of God's abundant generosity and goodness, giving away the grace that has been so freely lavished upon you, bringing joy to those you serve and glory to the one who has called you by name.

Let it be!

APPENDIX

How many spiritual gifts are there?

I think the number of gifts is, to some degree, a moot point. In my opinion, a more healthy perspective is to ask how is a gift being used and to determine if using it promotes unity in the body and glory to God.

For completeness, here is my summary list of the gifts I have examined in this book.

Romans 12

prophecy, service, one who teaches, one who exhorts, one who contributes (giving), leading, acts of mercy/ compassion, utterance of wisdom, utterance of knowledge, prophecy, distinguishing between spirits, various kinds of tongues, interpretation of tongues, helping, administration/guidance, healings, miracles

Ephesians 4

apostles, prophets, evangelists, shepherd, teacher

1 Corinthians 12

Message of wisdom; message of knowledge; faith; gifts of healing; miraculous powers; prophecy; distinguishing between spirits; speaking in different kinds of tongues; interpretation of tongues; helping; administration/guidance;

1 Corinthians 7.7

Gift of celibacy (& gift of being married?),

Ephesians 3.7

minister of the Gospel (or gift of God's grace?)

1 Peter 4.9-11

speaking oracles of God, serving, showing hospitality(?),

Hebrews 2.4

signs, wonders & miracles (or gift of Holy Spirit?)

ENDNOTES

[1] This may be an oxymoron to my American readers. In the USA, Baptists are not generally know for being theologically charismatic.

[2] Martin H. Manser, *Christian Quotations*, Accordance electronic ed. (London: Martin H. Manser, 2016), paragraph 11564.

[3] Henri Nouwen *The Return of the Prodigal Son* (Doubleday 1992)

[4] Martin H. Manser, *Christian Quotations*, Accordance electronic ed. (London: Martin H. Manser, 2016), paragraph 4396.

[5] This story is widely circulated on the internet with minor variations. Its origin is unknown.

[6] Fleming Rutledge, *'The Crucifixion: Understanding the Death of Jesus Christ'* (William B Eerdmans, GrandRapids 2015) p219.

[7] N.T. Wright, *'Paul for Everyone: 1 Corinthians'* (Westminster John Knox press, 2011)

[8] All three words are used in various English language translations

[9] Kenneth Bailey, *'The Poet and the Peasant'* (William B Eerdmans. Grand Rapids, 1976)

[10] Modalism is an easy heresy to fall into, but it is a heresy none the less.

[11] James G Dunn, *'The Theology of the Apostle Paul'* 1998. p437

[12] JI Packer, *'Knowing God'* p232

[13] JI Packer, *'Knowing God'* p236

[14] Martin H. Manser, *Christian Quotations*, Accordance electronic ed. (London: Martin H. Manser, 2016), paragraph 11654.

[15] 'A GREEK - ENGLISH LEXICON of the NEW TESTAMENT and other EARLY CHRISTIAN LITERATURE' 3rd EDITION (BDAG) revised and edited by Frederick William Danker.
    "προφητεία," 889.

[16] 1 Thess 5.19

[17] Martin H. Manser, *Christian Quotations*, Accordance electronic ed. (London: Martin H. Manser, 2016), paragraph 4362.

[18] Geoffrey W Bromiley, *Theological Dictionary of the New Testament (Abridged)*, (William B Eerdmans, Grand Rapids, 1985)

[19]https://www.ted.com/talks/simon_sinek_why_good_leaders_make_y-ou_feel_safe/transcript

[20] For the astute reader, you will notice that Paul actually slightly misquotes Ps 68.18. This is not the only time he does this, and the point is that he is pulling on OT imagery to help explain a truth, not necessarily that he is trying to make an OT prophecy 'fit'.

[21] Here I am indebted to Andrew Dowsett for his writing on 'people as gifts'. You can find his fine work at dowsetts.blogspot.com

[22] DNA stands for DeoxyriboNucleic Acid and is the molecule contained in every living cell that contains the genetic blueprint for each living species. It is passed down during reproduction.

[23] I belong to a church stream that is comfortable with appointing individuals to these offices so I am not against this at all. But I am passionate that every member of the body discovers what their Jesus DNA is and is discipled and activated in it.

[24] Mark Tubbs writes an excellent chapter on the subject of 'roles vs titles' in his very readable book '*The Five Fingers of God: Discovering Your Destiny through the Fivefold Gifts*'.

[25] Remember that the greatest is the least and the leader is the one who serves (Luke 22.25).

[26] Geoffrey W Bromiley, *Theological Dictionary of New Testament (Abridged)*. 69.

[27] ἀπόστολος, *BDAG Greek Lexicon*. 122

[28] All this seems to point to the reality that apostles are not defined simply as those who wrote scripture, nor that there were only twelve of them. Rather there were 12 particular Apostles who were personally called, discipled and sent by the risen Christ, and that does make them different from modern day apostles, but through his Spirit Jesus continues to call and send people today.

[29] The latin equivalent of *apostolos* is *Missio,* from which we get our English word *mission.*

[30] Again, I refer the reader to Mark Tubbs treatment of this topic in this book *Five Fingers of God.*

[31] Alan Hirsch *The Forgotten Ways* (Brazos Press, Grand Rapids 2006), 152.

[32] Michael Frost and Alan Hirsch *The Shaping Of Things To Come* (Hendrickson, Mass. 2003), 169.

[33] Michael Brodeur, *'Destiny Finder'* (Quintessant Media 2015) 84.

[34] The fancy name for this is 'Missio Dei'

[35] Note this ascension gift is a person. It differs from the gift of prophecy referred to in Romans and Corinthians

[36] You can read this story in Acts 17.15-34

[37] Hebr 13.20; 1 Peter 5.2-4

[38] JR Woodward, *Creating a Missional Culture* (InterVarsity Press 2012) *163*

[39] Andrew Dowsett has written a helpful description on each of the 20 primary APEST combinations in his paper *JesusGiven - living the life you were called to* available on his blog page.

[40] Che Ahn, *When Heaven Comes Down,* (Chosen Books 2009).

[41] I am really only commenting on the part of Christ's church that I have experience of. I am not suggesting that no other part of the Church through history has identified or embraced this fivefold DNA. The great Nicene creed of the Councils of Constantinople and Nicaea declare that there is only one Holy Catholic [universal] *apostolic* Church.

[42] I am indebted to conversations and interactions with several people in informing and stimulating my thinking in this area, specifically Michael Brodeur, Alex and Hannah Absalom, Ben Sternke, Dr Mark Virkler and my own colleagues on the Harvest Rock church leadership team.

[43] Martin H. Manser, *Christian Quotations*, Accordance electronic ed. (London: Martin H. Manser, 2016), paragraph 5646.

[44] Martin H. Manser, *Christian Quotations*, Accordance electronic ed. (London: Martin H. Manser, 2016), paragraph 11664.

[45] A great resource is *The Essential Guide to Healing* co-authored by Randy Clark and Bill Johnson.

[46] While it is a sacred Jewish text, and is included in the Old Testament canon for the Greek Orthodox and Roman Catholic churches, the Protestant Church gave it Apocryphal status. In any event, it gives an insightful perspective on healing that would be close to that of Jesus' first Jewish believers.

[47] 'Dancing hand' is the literal meaning of the word 'manifestation'

[48] John Arnott, *The Father's Blessing* (Charisma House. Lake Mary, 1995). p135

[49] Dr Mark Stibbe, *The Presents of God, Discovering your Spiritual Gifts.* (Authentic. Milton Keynes, 2014)